Art of the Monologue

MW00881710

Frank Catalano

ISBN: 1-4196-6834-X
ISBN-13: 9781419668340
Library of Congress Control Number: 2008908326

To order additional copies, please contact us.
BookSurge Publishing
www.booksurge.com

FORWARD

I have had the opportunity to teach acting for stage and camera over twenty years. During this time, I have always found it a challenge to find one comprehensive monologue textbook which contained the appropriate performance materials for college level students. Many of the existing texts contain selections from well-known staples of American and European drama. Other texts are compilations of materials written specifically as individual monologues geared more toward auditions than performance. I often suggest at the beginning of each semester that students purchase texts from a list of recommended but not required paperbacks so that they would have the best possible sources of material to meet their particular needs and to fully participate in the class. The problem with this scenario is that it is not cost effective for students to purchase a group of text books that they may or may not use during the course of the semester. In most Beginning classes specific monologues are assigned. However, at the Intermediate and Advanced level, the students want to have the ability to select material. This is often easier said than done because students often start one monologue and then abandon it for another. The end result, is that many students spend an inordinate amount of time pouring over the various texts researching and selecting material. Many times assignments due dates are often presented unprepared with the excuse: I couldn't find anything that was right for me. Many classes use improvisation to build student skill levels, inspire confidence and encourage creativity in performance.

The difficulty here is that many students (despite skill level) have the tendency to confuse improvisation with trying to be funny. Instead of focusing on the who, what, when and whereof a particular improvisation, they try to come up with the funniest lines or gestures. This can make for a wonderfully creative and fun class, but it also alienates those students that are not as adept with one liners as others. So while I do encourage the use of improvisation as a means to inspire creative choices, I feel the sooner students become familiar with handling varied types of scripted materials, the better. I enable them early on, to acquire interpretive skills and face the apprehension of memorization. The use of the monologue is a great way to start.

CLASSROOM/STUDIO TEXT

The individual pieces contained in this monologue volume or the parallel scene volumes are not created as part of any larger written well known body of work with linear plot lines. The construction here is compartmental with each piece existing on its own but connected thematically to the other 51. This type of construction allows both the instructor and the student the greatest amount of flexibility toward interpretation and performance. Students are encouraged to focus on the particular moments at hand and create a compelling reality within the parameters of each piece. In addition, each monologue has been created with the acting studio in mind. Settings and props are minimal to simplify the production requirements of each piece. The goal is for the student to focus on the particular acting requirements of each piece without the distraction of attempting to produce the technical aspects of a scene.

This collection of monologues when used as a classroom/ studio text can easily be accessed by genre, gender and age range. Attributes are approximate suggestions based upon the individual subjects and point of view of each monologue. In addition, students may select monologues by a particular acting objective, emotional attribute, singing, movement or dialect. These identified attributes make it easier for a particular student to work on a specific area of their craft.

THEATRICAL PRODUCTION

This volume may also be used as a full length script for presentation as theatrical production with the title FIFTY TWO PICKUP. The monologues both verse and prose are connected thematically as parts of life and time jumbled together like a deck of cards. Fifty-two cards in a deck and fifty-two weeks in a year of a life. The material is so arranged that any number of actors can be assigned specific monologues. I have included in the text a sample breakdown by gender and age for a cast of six. However, it can be divided any number of ways to accommodate a particular class or group of students. The instructor or director is not forced with those tough decisions of whom to cast in the lead role. Every actor in the class or group will be able to perform in accordance with their skill level while being part of the overall production. The material is designed to be presented within almost any staging configuration (Proscenium, Thrust or Round) with minimal props and set. Optional title placards can be presented before each monologue. Certain monologues are related by character or plot lines to allow for advanced students to create a larger character arc. These associated monologues are indicated in the MONOLOGUE ATTRIBUTES section of the text.

AUDITION MATERIAL

Lastly, the material in this volume may also be utilized as audition material. Some of the monologues are no longer than one minute in length and are designed to do on the spot with little or no physical preparation in an audition setting. The actor may choose the material by GENDER AND AGE RANGE. This will provide the casting personnel or agent the opportunity to see the actor perform material that is exactly the right fit for their particular casting type. The material can be presented as both contemporary and period formats. It is available in both prose and verse to offer casting personnel a fresh new set of material rather than the monologues they have heard so many times before. This fresh new approach will allow them to focus in on the performer's talent rather than have them compare an actor's particular performance with another actor who performed the same material.

CONTENTS

MONOLOGUE SELECTIONS

MONOLOGUE SELECTION CRITERIA:

HOW TO USE THIS BOOK

Use this book as both a reference source and work book. As a **reference source,** you may use any number of the monologues contained here as a source for studio work, audition material and for full performance opportunities. The **Monologue Attributes** section of the text will assist you in selecting the appropriate material for your particular needs.

As a **workbook,** this volume may be used to explore the intellectual, emotional and physical attributes of a monologue. Each monologue line is numbered in the left hand column of the page. The right hand column of each monologue has space lines so that each beat may be marked to indicate a specific intellectual, emotional or physical action. I encourage you to use the lined spaced and numbered portions of these pages to make personal notes, mark beats and make any marks that may assist you in creating the most compelling monologue performances you can imagine.

Monologue Assignment Sheets (Addendum #9)
Monologue Assignment sheets useful tools to assist actors in specifying particular goals for a class assignment, audition, or performance. As a studio tool, Assignment Sheets may be handed in to the class leader or teacher at time of performance. This will provide the teacher with a universal tool to identify

the student's goals and choices made for the assignment. In addition, it is a useful tool for the teacher to make notes for student improvement and artistic growth.

WHAT IS A MONOLOGUE?

The American Heritage Dictionary defines a monologue as a long speech made by one person, often monopolizing a conversation. You may be thinking, I already know *that*, tell me something I don't know. Okay, a monologue is really a small part of a character's soul. Think of those thoughts in which you have spoken out loud to someone or yourself. The words you utter come from within you and have special meaning. Unless, you count as monologues leaving phone messages, placing your order at the automated machine at Jack in the Box or trying to talk on the phone to Customer Service at your bank. So it's true that a monologue is a speech made by one person but really it's a lot more than just that. What the person says in his/her speech should be worthy of speech itself to be considered a monologue. What am I saying? It should be a speech connected in some core way to your character's intellectual, emotional and physical state. If it is not **that**, then it's not a monologue. It *is* whatever it is: leaving a phone message, ordering a cheeseburger or trying to find out why your check has bounced. But, what it is **not,** is a monologue. If we agree that a monologue is a speech made by one person and that the words spoken are connected to that person's intellectual, emotional and physical state, then let's look at the various types of monologues and how each should be considered.

WHAT TYPES OF MONOLOGUES ARE THERE?

Dramatic or comedic soliloquy

Your character speaks to themselves out loud

This is a dramatic device used to convey the inner thoughts of a character outwardly so that the audience may hear them. In short, the character talks about what they are thinking to themselves, out loud. Shakespeare uses this device when Macbeth contemplates murdering King Duncan. Macbeth debates the merits of killing Duncan, his friend and king:

Hautboys and torches. Enter a Sewer, and divers Servants with dishes and service, and pass over the stage. Then enter MACBETH

MACBETH

If it were done when 'tis done, then 'twere well
It were done quickly: if the assassination
Could trammel up the consequence, and catch
With his surcease success; that but this blow
Might be the be-all and the end-all here,
But here, upon this bank and shoal of time,

We'ld jump the life to come. But in these cases
We still have judgment here; that we but teach
Bloody instructions, which, being taught, return
To plague the inventor: this even-handed justice
Commends the ingredients of our poison'd chalice
To our own lips. He's here in double trust;
First, as I am his kinsman and his subject,
Strong both against the deed; then, as his host,
Who should against his murderer shut the door,
Not bear the knife myself. Besides, this Duncan
Hath borne his faculties so meek, hath been
So clear in his great office, that his virtues
Will plead like angels, trumpet-tongued, against
The deep damnation of his taking-off;
And pity, like a naked new-born babe,
Striding the blast, or heaven's cherubim, horsed
Upon the sightless couriers of the air,
Shall blow the horrid deed in every eye,
That tears shall drown the wind. I have no spur
To prick the sides of my intent, but only
Vaulting ambition, which o'erleaps itself
And falls on the other.

When he speaks, Macbeth is alone within the context of the play. However, the truth of it is that he speaks these thoughts in front of the audience. The audience, at once, knows Macbeth's torment about the king and what is to happen in the play. More importantly, the audience sees and hears it from Macbeth's own heart. Then, they watch it unfold the rest of the play.

A soliloquy can also be comedic. For example, the Porter's soliloquy in Macbeth in Act II, scene 3, Shakespeare has written a comic soliloquy at the very moment after Macbeth's murder of Duncan. There is a knock at the door. A sleepy and perhaps drunk porter shuffles into the room to answer.

Knocking within. Enter a Porter
Porter
Here's a knocking indeed! If a
man were porter of hell-gate, he should have
old turning the key.
Knocking within
Knock,
knock, knock! Who's there, I' the name of
Beelzebub? Here's a farmer, that hanged
himself on the expectation of plenty: come in
time; have napkins now about you; here
you'll sweat for't.
Knocking within
Knock, knock! Who's there, in the other devil's
name? Faith, here's an equivocator, that could
swear in both the scales against either scale;
who committed treason enough for God's sake,
yet could not equivocate to heaven: O, come
in, equivocator.
Knocking within
Knock,
knock, knock! Who's there? Faith, here's an
English tailor come hither, for stealing out of
a French hose: come in, tailor; here you may
roast your goose.
Knocking within
Knock,
knock; never at quiet! What are you? But
this place is too cold for hell. I'll devil-porter
it no further: I had thought to have let in
some of all professions that go the primrose
way to the everlasting bonfire.

Knocking within
Anon, anon! I pray you, remember the porter.
Opens the gate

I selected this soliloquy to illustrate two points, one that it is the character's thoughts and secondly that although it is comedic it frames a dramatic circumstance involving murder. Bottom line, not all comedic soliloquies are humorous to the characters who speak them.

Key characteristics of soliloquy
- Character reveals their inner thoughts, motives or intentions out loud
- Character talks to himself or herself
- Can be dramatic or comedic

Key Performance Attributes of soliloquy
The act of talking to one self is an illusion. Though your character believes they are alone, the reality is that the audience and perhaps another character is listening. Speak from your heart as if the words you utter have never been spoken until this moment in just this way. What ever is spoken in a soliloquy must be true. At least true reflection of the character's belief's and core values.

Dramatic or Comedic Monologue

Character talks to another character or to the audience as a character

This type of monologue can be presented in two different formats: **Representational** where the reality of the character or performer is different from the audience. In this case the character or performer does not interact or acknowledge the audience. This is often used by playwrights in monologues where one character confides in another and they are supposedly alone on the stage. However, the reality of the situation is that the audience is listening as well, and a plot point is conveyed.

The second format is **Presentational** where the reality of the character or performer is the same as the audience. In this case, the character or performer acknowledges and interacts with the audience as a character. This is sometimes used in theater and film where one character speaks a monologue to another character and then turns and gives an aside to the audience. Shakespeare and Moliere do it often in their plays and film makers such as John Hughes in FERRIS BUELLER's DAY OFF and Mel Brooks in BLAZING SADDLES, YOUNG FRANKENSTEIN and HISTORY OF THE WORLD PART I. In each case, the characters are in the middle of giving a speech to another character when they turn to the audience or camera and deliver an aside. Mel Brook's King Louis turns to camera after looking at a woman's breasts and says: It's good to be King! This is an aside.

Whether the monologue is delivered to another character or to the audience as a character, it is often used by writers as a dramatic device to advance the plot of the story. The monologue conveys the thoughts of one character to another character or to the audience directly. The monologues reveal some hidden quality of character or detail some past event. Many times in film, monologues are introduced through a combination of voice over and visual flashback. This provides a visual rendering of the monologue to the audience. The key factor in performing a monologue to another character or audience as a character is that their presence in some way must have a bearing on what is spoken and how it is conveyed. In short, the words and thoughts conveyed in monologue should create the other character visually in the imagination of the audience. This is even true if the monologue is directed toward the audience themselves. They way the character addresses the audiences, tells them a little about who they are supposed to be and ultimately how they are to react to the situation. How is this done? Every audience, once included in the reality of a character becomes a character itself and can be assigned attributes such as rich, poor, rabble, intellectual etc. When Puck, in the final monologue of Shakespeare's MIDSUMMER's NIGHTS DREAM, speaks at the end of the play who is he actually speaking to?

If we shadows have offended
Think but this, and all is mended
While these visions did appear
And this weak and idle theme,
No more yielding but a dream
Gentles, do not reprehend:
if you pardon, we will mend:
and, as I am an honest Puck
IF we have unearned luck
Now to escape the serpent's tongue,
We will make amends ere long:
Else Puck a liar call;
So, good night unto you all!

Further, is it the character Puck or the performer playing Puck actually speaking? Or both? And who is being spoken to? The audience? And what is their role in the play. Are they the rabble of the pit, a small gathering of nobility or is this a private performance for the Queen? Certainly, Puck is not speaking to his fellow Elizabethans. He is speaking to an audience whom he hopes will be pleased with his passing, he hopes not to offend and ultimately gain some favor from. Perhaps it is nobility. The very lines themselves and the way they are delivered create an image of the audience in our minds. The creation of the who in a monologue where you are speaking to someone, is essential for the piece to ring true, even if the who is the audience themselves.

In the text, **Monologue #7 CRIME**, the audience the character addresses is large group of high school students on graduation day. The challenge of the performer is to create the enthusiasm, spontaneity and youthful irreverence of a group of seventeen year old high school students to make the monologue work. This is accomplished with both physicality, and emotional connection. The speaker of the monologue must see this audience create a physical and emotional reaction to the audience to make his words carry weight.

The reason why I came here is to talk about tomorrow. I see you sitting here today all pumped up about getting out of here and making some wild ass future for yourself. And that's great! That's the way it should be! When you get out there, the world is going to be wonderful adventure and it's going to be a pain in the ass too. It's also going to be harsh and cold and too expensive, too crowded and sometimes you will want to chuck it all. But you won't... that would be a crime. Instead, you'll deal with it calmly... and make the world better place. I want you all to promise me that ... make the world a better place... not just the words. I want you **really** to do it... or that would really be a crime. Do it for yourself (Beat) and do it for Johnny.

Without the creation of an audience, this monologue could become a lonely brother's angry letter to the world. However, with the creation of the audience of young students full of hope and tomorrow, we somehow begin to see the tragedy and loss of the situation.

Key characteristics - Monologues spoken to other characters and audience as a character
- Character talks to other characters or audience
- Character and Performer creates a visual image and emotional response the characters being spoken to
- Can be dramatic or comedic.

Key Performance Attributes - Monologues spoken to other characters and audience as a character

Creating a visual image of the character or audience as a character. React to who you are speaking to even though they may not speak. In actuality, the character you speak to is an illusion and will become real only if you physically and emotionally react to them. One you stop seeing them, they will vanish in the eyes of the audience.

As in a soliloquy, speak from your heart as if the words you utter have never been spoken in just this way.

Stand-Up Comedy Monologue

Series of written jokes or comic scenarios
Performed by a comedian to a live audience

Stand-Up comedy centers on a **comedian** or **stand-up comic** who performs directly to a live audience with the ultimate goal of making the audience laugh. The comedic monologue can have a formal written structure with a beginning, middle and end or be based upon a free form scenario or improvisational structure. The formal written structure is usually a list of jokes or set ups performed in a specific order designed to complete the monologue in a fixed time frame ending with a crescendo. The free form scenario or improvised structure is usually based upon general areas the comedian wants to explore. Often the approach to the material is prompted by audience suggestions and interaction.

The Stand-up monologue is performed live on stage, with a microphone and possibly a stool. The key dynamic of stand-up is that it requires a live audience. Could you imagine Jay Leno doing his stand-up monologue alone in a room in front of the camera. The audience is the essential ingredient for stand-up comedy to function.

The monologues are performed directly to the audience and the comedian can be themselves or take on the persona of various characters. In some instances, stand up monologues can contain dialogues between more than one character. In this case, the stand-up comedian creates each character using a different vocal quality, physicality and emotional state. This works well as long as the audience is clearly aware who each character is and when they are speaking. The subject matter of most stand-up monologues is contemporary topics including current events, politics, famous personalities and generic situations such as family, friends, marriage, dating and work. Some stand-up monologues can tackle serious issues but they have to find that fine line getting the point across without getting too didactic. The key factor in performance of stand-up monologues is audience stand-up performer chemistry. It is essential for the performer to have some type of connection with the audience almost immediately upon entering the room. The stand up comedian must acknowledge the audience from the very first moments of the monologue. It can be a simple as just saying hello, how you all doing out there tonight? Or commenting on something or an event that is in the public consciousness. For example, the traffic, the weather or whatever was on the front page that day. This gives the audience the feeling that you are with them, you breathe the same air, move in the same space and have the same concerns they do. Jay Leno is a master at audience connection. No matter what the quality of his material on any particular show, he makes it work. He even gets a laugh on the bad jokes by commenting on them and making fun of himself. The audience can help but like him because he is a mirror image of a part of all of us. We want him to succeed and we laugh with him because he is part of us. Other comedians such as Kathy Griffin, or the late Rodney Dangerfield take on a specific stance in society. Griffin's My Life on the D List, creates a persona who shows us the over indulgent hypocritical world of celebrities and Dangerfield created a kind of every man who never got any respect. In each case, these stand-up performers found a way to identify with their audience, make them feel comfortable and ultimately to laugh.

Key Characteristics of stand up comedy monologue
- Live audience in which audience often participates
- Usually performed with a microphone and possibly a stool

- Communicated to the audience through spoken word and occasionally song.
- Can be communicated in first person or through created characters

Key Performance Attributes of stand-up comedy monologue
- First, acknowledge the audience as soon as possible
- Second, identify with the audience as soon as possible even if it means making fun of yourself. When a joke or bit doesn't work acknowledge it. You don't have to write your own material to be a stand-up comic

Example from this text: #40 COFFEE PEOPLE (MALE)
(ENTER holding cup of coffee) How's everybody doing tonight? Tough day eh? Me too? That's why I stopped off for a little pick me up on the way here. Helps me put on the edge. No, not drugs! (Takes a sip). I'm talking about a cup of coffee, rich, dark, full bodied… warms me up all over. (SIP) Nothing like it… There are two kinds of people in the world. Tea People and Coffee People. Tea People are usually left wing tree hugging Green Peacers that think by drinking their decaf chai mint tea espressos that they're saving the planet. They tell you that Coffee People are hopped up caffeine freaks that don't have a clue about the world. They will get on their tea box and preach to you that coffee people have no idea where coffee comes from and that millions of poverty stricken people in third world countries work long hours growing and picking coffee earning as little as a penny per pound. They look at you smugly and say How can you drink that cup of coffee obtained by exploitation of the masses! Those are the Tea People.

(Beat) I'm in the second group, the Coffee People. While we're aware of the socioeconomic and political conditions on the planet, we are not consumed them. To us, Coffee is not just a drink… It's an experience that represents the passage of time with friends or loved ones... a physical state of being and more importantly a philosophy of life. Yes, it's true to be a coffee person is to know extreme ecstasy that can be found when you take your first morning whiff of a full bodied, earthy and dark and ferociously brewed cup of morning coffee. From the first sip you are transported on a mystical journey to the rustic rain drenched mountains of the old country where Juan Valdez (his head covered by a sombrero so as to not get too much sun) carefully hand picks each Columbian bean and places it gently in a hemp sack strapped to the back of his loyal donkey. I've seen his picture on the can of coffee. Valdez doesn't look exploited to me? In fact, he seems pretty damn happy... and don't I deserve a little bit of happiness? So, I take another sip... it's perfect... and at that very moment in time, there is nothing else in the universe except me and my cup of coffee. This is life at its fullest and the world is bright and full of possibilities. (Beat, Drinks from cup)

As you drink, you feel it rushing through your veins... empowering you... bringing clarity where there was none...priming you like a pump... winding you tighter and tighter - you're almost there... a pulsating - throbbing ball of energy ready to explode off the launch pad like a rocket blasting off to the moon!

(Gulps remainder of the cup down, then calmly)

Now... I'm ready to face the day. (EXITS). You could also add, an acknowledgment of the audience with the line. Thank you, good night!

Short story or Narrative

Conversion of literature to performance medium

These can be performed both in first and third person with source material usually from longer forms including novels, anthologies and short fiction. Performers who choose to develop this form of monologue must never forget that the original intent of the author was to have the material read not spoken in the presence of a live audience. You may ask, what's the difference? The imagery used in written fiction for example relies on the imagination of the reader to create the characters, emotions and visual images in the story. When this type of material is converted for use in film or the stage, a whole different sensory dynamic is in play. The audience is watching and listening. The visual imagery and characterization work is all done for them. However, if the writing is still the same, it may come into conflict with the actual live or filmed presentation. There is also the issue of run time. In literary fiction there is a totally different concept of time and audience. There is no fixed time frame to tell the story and often the arc of the character takes place over hundreds of pages. In the live theater or film and in the presentation of a monologue for performance, the amount of time available is finite. You may have no more than two to three minutes to get the job done. That's it.

So what is to be done? The easy answer is for audition purposes, avoid these types of monologues. The more creative answer is if you love the piece and it reveals something unique about your acting ability, then do it. However, with that said, you have to find a way to present the piece so that it comes alive off the page and works within the theatrical or film mediums.

Edit for time, continuity and sense. The piece should be shortened to one to three minutes and contain a character arc, emotion and physicality that can conveyed to an audience within the limitations of presentation. If it sounds good when read off the page, conjures within your imagination wonderful imagery but loses all of this in the translation, then I'd say don't do it. But, if you are able to convey the full power of the work and showcase your talent in the process, this is the piece for you.

Note: Many monologue texts and notations from casting director's personal list in their many do's and don'ts of monologues - Don't do a narrative! I don't and won't say that, if the material works for you and shows your talent, then go for it. It's time we break the old cliché's of do's and don'ts and start thinking about the art form and the actor. If you can be wonderful, it doesn't matter what material you perform, they will only remember your performance.

Key Characteristics of short story or narrative
- Material derived from longer narrative form including novels, anthologies and short fiction
- Most contain visual imagery, emotion and a physical state written to be read not performed.

Key Performance Attributes of short story or narrative
- Must be edited down for stage or film performance (1-3 minutes)
- Must contain a character arc, emotional state and physicality

Monologue #47 CHICKEN (MALE)
It is essential that the performer of this rather long piece have an effective strategy of creating a character arc for both the

narrator of the monologue and the voice of chicken. In addition, the piece is narrated as a flashback where both characters speak to one another within the monologue. It must be made clear to the audience which character is speaking as well as what is going on within any given moment of the narrative.

In addition, the performer is challenged to create a visual image of Chicken's father who is instrumental to understanding who Chicken is and why he does what he does. How is this to be accomplished?

In the annotation portion of your text, mark out those beats where Chicken speaks and the other parts where the narrator is speaking. Look at each character separately and try to determine an arc for each of the characters. Once an arc is established for each character, the performer can return to the logistics of presentation.

How can this be broken down into character arcs?

SEE EXAMPLE BELOW:

Character: Chicken in BLACK

Character: Narrator in *ITALIC*

When I was sixth grade halfway between boy and man, I had a friend in my class. His name was Chicken. That wasn't his real name... but the kids in the class used to call him Chicken. Chicken was a freckle faced, lanky stick of a kid with a bush of red hair on top of his head. He had a hard time fitting into his wooden desk because his legs were too long. We used to say he had long chicken legs... but that's not how he got the name Chicken ... and yeah ... he did have a real name, Jacob Lucas. But no one except our teacher Mr. Garvey ever called him Jacob. To us, he was just Chicken.

(BEAT) Chicken came into our class about the middle of the school year. Mr. Garvey brought him in to the class and said something like *Now boys and girls, I want you to say hello to our new classmate who just moved here from West Virginia. Say hello Jacob ! Nobody really knew where West Virginia was as we sang out H E L L O J A C O B. Then, Mr. Garvey continued: Now Jacob, tell us something about yourself. The poor kid looked like he was going to pass out. His face got redder than his hair and he started sweating then he stood up tall like he was facing a firing squad, took a deep breath and cleared his throat.*

Jacob Lucas... that's my Christian name after my dad ... and my grandfather before him ... think the Lucas's came to West Virginia from Ireland ... even thing one or two of em scrapped with Indians in the French and Indian War.

That was the first time I heard a West Virginia accent. He went on: Jacob Lucas that what it sez on paepers an'all ... but I go by the name Chicken. My Dad started it cause he said I like to run so much ... Ya`know like a crazy chicken. I got mad at first, but then, I kinda got used to it ... suppose Dad figured right that chicken was a fittin name to find out who yer friends ire ... and make ya tough enough to take care yer enemies ... if ya have anny. So, Jacob Lucas's my name ... and y'can call me that but everybody that's my friend ... calls me Chicken. Ya`know like the bird.

There were a few giggles followed by silence Chicken looked out over the room: Any Questions? Lucy Sullivan, pulled on one of her pigtails when she raised her hand: What's West Virginia like?

(BEAT) *Chicken thought for a moment then said:* If you could close yer eyes and imagine Heaven right here on this earth, I spect that's West Virginia. My Dad and I lived on this farm down Putnam

County ways. Mom died was I was born ... never met her, so it was jest him en me. Our farm is between the railroad tracks and the river ... nothin to hollar at ... just a small patch a dirt and green. I went to Bunker Hill Schewl ... near the mines ... that is till Dad got sick with some kinda cancer. Then, I couldn't go to schewl much ... had to take care of the farm... weren't too bad ... that is till Dad got sicker and ... then he died. He's all I had... that and a second cousin ... living up here. The room became still and Chicken looked over at Mr. Garvey to show him where he should sit. When Susan Sullivan sat up straight and said: Tell us more. Chicken hesitated: Not too much more ta tell ... exceptin maybe the day my Dad died... I was cryin next ta him lyin in bed en all en dedn't want to be an orphan an I asked him what was I goin ta do... He whispered in my ear. Son, don't matter what'ya plant ... it's how ya plow the field and make it grow. I never quite rightly knew what he did mean... being that he passed right after he told me. Guess I'll figure it'all out someday when I get older and such. Seein as this my first day a school and all... I kinda thinka ya'all as my freinds... and that bein so... and ya'll lettin me jabber up here ... I'll be yer friend as well ... for life.

So ya'll can call me Chicken! *(BEAT) ...and that's what we called him Chicken. Chicken went to the same school as I did right through high school. He was my best friend. Whenever I needed anything, Chicken was always there. In our senior year, he was the top running back on our school football team. I guess his father was right... Chicken loved to run when he got the ball he just took off and there wasn't much anybody could do to stop him... scouted by all the colleges for a scholarship.*
(BEAT) That was until he started to change. It was hardly noticeable at first ... wasn't as fast as he used to be and was tired all the time. Then, he got worse. (BEAT) I remember the day he went to the hospital. We'll fight and beat this! He looked me in the eye and said: We sure will! But he didn't. (BEAT) Chicken died four months later...

I wanted him to fight… fight for his life but he just wouldn't do it. He died. I lived.

(BEAT) And for a long time, I was very angry at Chicken… for dying … and because he seemed to just accept his fate. He knew he was going to die and he seemed so content with it. Some people work their whole lives chasing their dreams and when they get it, they're still not happy. He never even had the chance. (BEAT) Now that time has passed, I think I understand. He savored every moment of it and fought to make what he had the best life possible. He truly lived until the day he died. No regrets.

(BEAT) Chicken, now I understand. Don't matter what ya plant… it's how ya plow the field… and make it grow.

CONTEMPORARY VS. CLASSICAL MONOLOGUES

Contemporary monologues refer to those pieces written after the realistic period approximately 1900. It doesn't mean, only those monologues written now.

CLASSICAL MONOLOGUES

Refer to classical plays of the Ancient Greeks (Euripides, Sophocles, Aeschylus) or Christopher Marlowe, William Shakespeare, John Webster, Lope de Vega, Beaumont & Fletcher, Moliere (in verse translation), Edmond Rostand, William Congreve, and Richard Brinsley Sheridan. Many of the monologues selected from plays by these authors will be in verse. The monologues contained in this volume are considered to be Contemporary and part of a larger theatrical play called 52 Pickup.

Lyrical or Verse Monologues

Most monologues are written in a conversational form of prose. That is ordinary speech patterns or dialects with a metrical type of structure or rhyming scheme. However, some monologues, mostly classical, are written in verse form. These monologues are written using a particular meter as the main organization of the words and ideas they contain. Elizabethan writers like William Shakespeare and Christopher Marlowe primarily used **Iambic pentameter** following, generally, a pattern of an unrhymed selection of dialogue which sounded like *da dum da-dum da-dum da-dum da-dum* (expressed in a pattern as (soft STRONG / soft STRONG / soft STRONG / soft STRONG / soft STRONG) so that when spoken out loud by an actor had a auditory flow similar to the human heart beat. For example Christopher Marlowe's famous quote from Dr. Faustus adheres to the iambic pentameter pattern:

Was-this the-face that-launch'd a-thou sand-ships
And-burnt the-top less-tow ers-of Il-ium?

With that said, not all verse you will perform will be in Iambic pentameter and not all verse can be considered as poetry. However, as a performer what you should consider is how language is used when reciting verse. Think of it not so much in the strict patterned telling *(da-dum da-dum da-dum da-dum da-dum)* but more in terms of the lyrical or musical quality of what you speak. Poetic language relies on visual metaphor and simile and often creates sections of dialogue which reduce the use of words to a minimum, but yet the performer doesn't have the luxury of having the audience ponder the metaphor. How do you play these type of monologues? The performer must make sense of it despite the metaphor and after sense is made, connect a certain physicality and emotional state.

All of the general elements of verse we have discussed still hold true but now added to the mix is the consideration that you are presenting within a writer's medium in which the highest most regarded parts are its language. If you were a painter, you would be concerned with color, texture and lines and as a performer creating a character in verse you are using language as a painter would use the strokes of a paint brush. Don't get caught in the trap of putting all your efforts in *how* you say it rather than the true meaning of the situation the words create. If you speak beautiful rhymes but don't find the appropriate interpretation you will have nothing to connect to and if you don't connect, the audience doesn't connect.

WHY IS IT IMPORTANT FOR ME TO STUDY MONOLOGUES?

As a classroom studio tool

A Monologue is an excellent medium for a studio teacher to evaluate a particular student's ability to perform a prepared (memorized) selection of material to demonstrate the actor's ability to on their own (without a director)

to create character

to create emotion

to create physicality

As a demonstration of talent and ability

(for casting or artistic representation)

Most casting directors want to see actors perform through cold readings or prepared scenes sides of the actual project they are being considered. Monologues are still used in general types of auditions where the auditioners (such as Agents, Conservatories, Artistic Companies and Artist Representatives) want to see the actor perform prepared selections of material. Why do they want to see prepared material as opposed to cold readings? I think they often want to see both. Seeing an actor perform a short monologue gives the them an opportunity to access the performer's ability to imaginatively produce a particular segment with a clear cut beginning, middle and end. They also, can observe the performer's approach to the role and get an idea of their commitment and talent. get an idea of their commitment and talent.

As a marketing tool to showcase a particular element of your talent.

All performers should have at least two monologues ready to go at all times. At least a comedy and a dramatic piece and for the more advanced actor both classical and contemporary dramatic and comedy monologues.

HOW DO I SELECT A MONOLOGUE THAT IS RIGHT FOR ME?

No matter how versatile you think you may be as a performer, a casting director or agent will only market your talent according to what they feel is your appropriate type.

By Casting Type

Type is a combination of factors which can include your: age, physical stature, hair color, ethnicity, speech patterns or accent and generally the way you appear to most people most of the time. You want to select a monologue that is type appropriate for you. That is, if you are female age twenties, you should not select an older woman. Pick someone generally your own age. Agents and casting directors will look to identify you in one type category or another.

By Talent and Skills

You want to select a monologue that will highlight what you do the best. If you have difficulty in showing intense emotion, then stay away from those types of monologues until you can perfect the skill to perform them. Select monologues that will highlight what you do best.

Compatibility with Career or Artistic Goals

Select monologues that are compatible with the goals you are attempting to achieve. If you are auditioning for a commercial agent, a crisp, short, high energy monologue would probably be best. A longer dramatic narrative or verse monologue would not be the best choice for a commercial agent, but may work in perfectly for an audition for a theater company or college.

Purpose or Skill Goal

Select a monologue towards working on a specific acting goal. For example, if you are asked to work on emotion, select a monologue that will stretch your abilities in that area.

USING THE MONOLOGUE ATTRIBUTE SECTION OF THIS BOOK

You can use the Monologue Attribute section as a tool to assist you in determining the best type of monologue for your particular goal. All of the monologues contained in this book take place in general settings with no more than one small hand held prop. Depending upon the intended purpose of the monologue class exercise, audition or full performance, you may wish to eliminate the prop all together.

The attribute section includes the following sections:

Genre
Drama or comedy

Gender/Age Range
Casting and type appropriateness for class exercises and Audition material selection.
Gender/Age Range
Young Male Teen - Twenties
Young Female Teen - Twenties
Adult Male - Thirties - Forties
Adult Female - Thirties - Forties
Adult Male - Forties and Up
Adult Female - Forties and Up

Objective

Suggests a specific acting and character objective to be achieved within the monologue

Emotional content

Highlights a certain emotionality and physical goal for the performer to work on in studio exercises.

Props

Indicates the specific prop requirements of the monologue.

Other General attributes including:

Character/plot linkages to other monologues in the text

Use of dialect

Use of music/dance

Lyric/Verse

Special use of physicality

HOW DO I PREPARE A MONOLOGUE FOR PRESENTATION?

AS A CLASS/STUDIO EXERCISE

Work closely with your studio teacher to determine personal creative acting goals within the class/studio setting. Ask the studio teacher which elements of performance you should be working on. For example, you may be asked to work on certain skills aimed at expanding certain emotional qualities. You can use the monologue attributes section to find the appropriate monologue to use to achieve this goal.

AS AN AUDITION PIECE

Selecting a monologue to be used as audition material should take into consideration first and foremost appropriate type and casting. In addition to these criteria, you will want to select a monologue which shows off you and your talent in the best way possible. Depending on your skill level, you should select a monologue that contains the appropriate attributes to show an agent or casting director your best work.

AS PART OF A LIVE THEATRICAL OR FILMED PERFORMANCE

The fifty two monologues that are contained in this collection can be presented as a full stage or film collection entitled 52 PICKUP. There is a suggested breakdown for a cast of six performers. However, the cast can be any size and the monologues can be assigned to as many performers that are available. The production presented would have no main or supporting performers but would be a true ensemble piece with limited requirements for sets, properties and lighting. This is an ideal collection for an advanced college studio or student production and can be presented both on stage and filmed formats.

IMPLEMENTATION STRATEGY FOR PRESENTING YOUR MONOLOGUE

WHAT IS AN IMPLEMENTATION STRATEGY?

Think of an implementation strategy as a plan to create a frame or foundation in to build your monologue. The implementation strategy becomes the concept for presentation. Whatever the purpose of your monologue presentation, your preparation for presentation should include an implementation strategy or plan of presentation. You may ask, it is the performer's job to create the character's physicality and emotion, why should I concern myself with the nuts and bolts of how it will be presented. The answer is the who and the how are indelibly connected. It's like the chef who labors over the preparation and ingredients put into a particular dish, forgetting presentation and just throws his creation onto a paper plate. In that very act, the chef negates everything that has been done. An actor is no different; consideration of presentation is just as important as preparation. While an actor can't control all aspects of presentation, the development of an implementation strategy will create a foundation for the actor to rely upon.

HOW DO I CREATE AN IMPLEMENTATION STRATEGY?

#1:   DISCOVERING A PRESENTATION DYNAMIC

Making a creative box to play in

The Dynamic of any presentation takes into consideration all of the physical characteristics of the performance space, the performer's relationship to that space, the distance of the intended audience to the performer, the composition of the intended audience, the surrounding reality of the performance and ultimately the purpose of the performance itself. The dynamics of any given performance can change as the physical characteristics of the performance space change. While it is virtually impossible for any performer to know totally the dynamic of every performance in advance. It is possible to develop a strategy of presentation, based upon what elements are available.

For a Classroom/Studio Assignment

You know the dynamics of this space whether it is round, proscenium or thrust staging, the lighting available and the distance you will be to the intended audience. In addition, you know the audience and the purpose of the performance is not only to entertain but to work on a specific element of your acting craft or to fulfill and assignment. Usually, the environment is relaxed and doesn't contain all of the production elements (lighting, music, costume etc) that a full out performance would contain.

For an Audition

In this case, you can only assume the dynamics of the space and distance to the intended audience. You might be asked to present your monologue in an office setting, a conference room, or an empty stage. The best strategy is to develop a plan for all three and be prepared for any variation you might encounter. Remember that in an audition dynamic that the person you are auditioning for may be looking for a specific element and not your total performance. They also may be multi tasking (making notations, conferring with an associate or looking at your resume) while you are in the midst of your performance. Lastly, the reality you attempt to create might be interrupted by an outside source such as a telephone, a person entering or the casting person themselves.

For a Full Production Performance
The most controlled of the three. Through rehearsal, you will become accustomed to the type of stage space, distance to the audience and production elements that should be considered when presenting your monologue. You may feel that this will fall on the director's job description, but remember not all directors will consider these elements. Some directors will let you develop your own blocking, physicality and character choices. Others will dictate every detail of what you are to do. You should prepare a strategy that will accommodate both methods and ensure that the character and presentation you make will be received fully by the audience within the dynamic of presentation.

#2.   CREATING A REALITY - USING WHO, WHAT WHERE AND WHEN
Develop a relationship between your character and monologue:
Who are you?

Personal
Are you married, divorced, single? Have a boyfriend or girlfriend or are you alone. Do you have any sort of attachment to any living entity, material thing or idea?

Professional

What do you do? Writer, fireman, nurse etc. and how do you feel about what you do? Do you tell everyone about it or do you hide it? What are you and what do you pretend to be?

Private

Something private about your character that no one else knows about. What do you fear? What do you do or say when there is no one around to listen? What secrets do you have that you won't ever tell anyone about? What do you really want out of life? Are you a liar?

Who are you talking to - Person, Place or Thing?

Outer circle: Someone you might or might not know

A stranger

Is it someone you have never spoken with before or perhaps only know from a distance. What is your impression of this person or thing and what does it think of you? What do you know about who or what you are talking to? Do you believe all of what you see, hear, smell, taste or touch about what or who you are talking to?

Acquaintance

Not your friend but someone you talk to from time to time. Perhaps a co worker, a waiter, the mailman, or dry cleaner. You deal with this person in a very narrow framework which might include Hello, Goodbye, I'll have a cheeseburger etc...

Superior Acquaintance

Someone you really don't know who has undue amount of influence over certain aspects of your being. Your boss, teacher, doctor, dentist or therapist.

Deified Acquaintance or Celebrity

Someone you don't know personally from experience but rather you know this person through external sources such as the television, film or newspapers. You know who this person or entity is but they may or may not know you at all. These type of people or entities could be celebrities, well known personalities and even Gods. They may or may not have an influence over your life.

Inner Circle: Someone you know well

A Friend

What kind of friend is this? Is it your best friend that you would tell anything to, or is it a distant friend someone or something you know of, but really don't share all of your feelings with.

Best Friend or Confidant

This is someone you would divulge any secret to and feel the most comfortable being with. A soul mate intellectually, emotionally and a physical mirror of your own persona.

Family Member

Someone in your blood circle including a mother, father, sister, brother, cousins, aunts, uncles etc. There is a certain familiarity or possibly contempt.

A Mentor

A person whom you look up to and want to emulate.

A Lover New from a distance

The highest state of awareness and care. Either heaven or hell, you want to please them or destroy them. You don't want their attention or long for it.

A Lover Present

The most intimate of all relationships could be wife husband, girlfriend or boyfriend. You want it or you don't or you are not sure which.

Lover Past

The root of the tree runs deep even though its branches have been cut. You play either the euphoria of the time it was new or the pain of it's end. A lover past can be either alive or deccased.

An Enemy

The closest of all relationships because you are consumed with their every breath, desire and move. Enemies can be loved, hated or envied.

Self: You speak to yourself

Self - (Auditory)

Soliloquy, You speak out loud to yourself. Can be accompanied with a certain physicality or activity.

Self - (Non Auditory)

You speak to yourself within your mind. This is usually accomplished through voice over and may be accompanied by a certain physicality or event. For example, you speak to your inner self while you drive the car, walk down the street, sit at a park bench. Also, used for narration of a story.

Imaginary

You speak to yourself either out loud or to your inner self (auditory/non auditory) to an imaginary character which can be an alter ego or one of any sub characters within your character.

What is going on at this moment?

At the very moment the monologue begins what is really happening. If you took a snapshot of this moment, what would be its title? If you enter the your home holding a bouquet of flowers, kiss your wife and hand them to her, and then after giving them to her, telling her that you have lost your job, what is the title under this moment? It can be called many things, perhaps losing or loss or love but it would not be called Handing her the bouquet because that action is not what is really going on. It is just an action which is part of the overall moment. So ask yourself, what is really going on at this moment in time, in your character's universe when your monologue begins.

When is this moment in time?

Once you have established what the true moment is than address the question is when is it. Using the example described above, the moment can be described as morning, day or night but more helpful would be the moment after I lost my job or late at night after I've been walking for hours, because I didn't know how I would tell you.

Where are you? What is the space?

Even though you may perform your monologue in any number of nondescript spaces, make a decision for your character about where this moment is taking place. Is it home, on the bus, in an elevator, on a podium in front of a thousand spectators? What is the space? Is it small and confined, larger than life or somewhere in between? Don't confuse this with the Dynamic of Performance (that is more concerned with the physical properties of the performance space) The where are you question addresses solely the reality of the character not the performance.

#3.   CREATING A MOMENT BEFORE

Where have you come from and What has just happened the moment before?

Within the reality of your character, what moment has the character just left before they entered the moment of your monologue. What was significant about that moment and how has the moment before influenced the intellectual, emotional and physical state of your character during the monologue.

#4.   CREATING NOW - CREATING SPECIFIC OBJECTIVES AND BEATS

What is your character's main objective?

By speaking the words of the monologue and living the moment, what does your character desire to have happen by the end of the scene?

What are your character's sub objectives or beats?

Are there smaller objectives or beats your character must achieve in order to achieve their main objective. A beat could be a small section of the dialogue or movement within the monologue.

What are the obstacles preventing you from reaching your character' sub objective's and main objective?

In the course of events leading up to, during and after the completion of the monologue, can you identify any obstacles which are preventing your character from achieving his/her desired goals? Are these obstacles generated externally (literally physical elements) or internal (obstacles created from within your character) that prevent them from their objective?

#5.   CREATING MOMENT AFTER

Where are you going to?

If your character is in a particular space in a particular moment, where will they go next. Perhaps nowhere, perhaps everywhere. Create a concept of motion. Let your words in the monologue and the life you have in the moments you create propel you to the next.

What's going to happen next?

Not asking you to predict the future. But your character and the audience in a larger sense should have some idea about where you are going in the next moment as a result of your uttering the words you have spoken. Everybody loves to peer into the future and know, if even briefly, what the next moment will bring. Even if you don't really have a clear cut idea of all of it, give your character and your audience a taste of what may come next.

NOW I HAVE AN IMPLEMENTATION STRATEGY - HOW DO I DO IT?

USING THE IMPLEMENTATION STRATEGY
AND MAKING SPECIFIC CHOICES TO ACHIEVE
A CREATIVE MONOLOGUE

#1   *PERFORMING WITHIN THE PRESENTATION DYNAMIC*

Play each moment as if it were a piece of a larger mosaic

The Presentation Dynamic is literally the creative box which is reality which makes up your character's world and the actual elements present within your specific performance environment all rolled into one. It could be a stage, a camera angle, a casting office, or on set location that your character must evolve within. Once you have established this creative box that your character lives within, you are free to explore the multitude of possibilities that are present within that dynamic at that moment in time. Using all that stimuli within the dynamic created forces your character to react to his/her universe rather than project the choices made by an actor. Your character is alive and reacting.

PRESENTATIONAL type monologues such as Stand Up Comedy rely heavily on the reality of the moment. Much of the reality of your character and presentation hinges on the energy and interaction with the audience. In this way, no joke or comic bit should ever be performed in a set manner. It will always be slightly different depending upon the unique combination of people that make up the audience, physical space created within that dynamic.

REPRESENTATIONAL types of monologue which are either dramatic or comedic also rely on the specific energy of the moment. In live theater, whether or not the audience responds to a specific line or in filmed performance depending on the camera angle or number of takes of a particular shot. Each time the character utters the words in a live performance on stage or within a take, they are slightly different because they are a response to the state of the presentation dynamic as it exists at that particular moment in time.

#2 CREATING A REALITY: USING WHAT IF?

Make specific choices using What if you have made the choices detailing who, what, where and when. Now, let your character ask him/herself the question: **What if** one of these choices weren't so? Example: You are Romeo quietly watching Juliet standing on her balcony.

Who: Romeo - A Montague (who falls in and out love) and enemy of the Capulets

What: Spying upon Juliet as she speaks her private thoughts

Where: The Capulet's orchard, Verona - a place he should not be.

When: Nighttime after the Capulet feast

Romeo sees the love of his life but cannot muster the will to speak? And with each line he falls deeper and deeper and succumbs to his fear and gets up to run away.

Then at the last possible moment, despite his fear, he hears Juliet say:

Romeo, doff thy name,
And for that name which is no part of thee
Take all myself!
When Romeo hears this, his fear, vanishes in an instant,
and he speaks! Why? He knows he can get it all.
I take thee at thy word:
Call me but love, and I'll be new baptized;
Henceforth I never will be Romeo

Using What if you are choosing to play the moment as if this time it will be different. You are playing this scene and speech as if he were going to walk away and somehow this play, at this moment in time is different than any other that has happened before. The key to playing the what if is that your character must believe and more importantly the audience must believe it. Fight the logical inclination to say to yourself: This is Shakespeare or this is the text, it cannot be changed. I am not suggesting a change in text, only a change in intention. We often play the end of the scene because there is a preconceived notion by both performers and audiences as to how it all turns out. We need to recreate that notion in the form of "what if." Let the audience sit on the edge of their seats and wonder if that maybe just this time at this moment, Romeo just might walk away. What would happen then? Using this approach makes your work unpredictable and interesting.

#3   *CREATING THE MOMENT BEFORE* - realistically playing the moment before your monologue begins

First of all, your monologue doesn't begin when your character first speaks. It is a broader stroke than that. Your monologue, is a slice of a much larger life, in which all that has gone before take it to the moment you now must play. When you begin your monologue give the audience a glimpse of that life before. Create a space - Ask yourself where was I before I was in this space? Have I just entered or has some new sensory stimulation occurred? If you have just entered, how is the new space different. What of the old space do you retain?

Example #1

If you come in from the cold to a warm space. Initially, you are still cold. After a while, your body becomes warm and the physicality reflects this. However, it is not an automatic or immediate transition. It is gradual.

Example #2:

You enter an elevator full of people. Where were you just the moment before? What is your character's attitude about that earlier moment? Then, you enter the elevator and have to change. Your physicality must adjust to the confined space and larger number of people.

Example #3: You enter the space and bring not a physical condition but an emotional one. In the previous moment, you learn that you have lost your job and now when you enter the new space you bring that emotion of loss with you.

Bringing in the moment before allows you to create a total present moment because the present is a compilation of all that has been and all that could be. So, how you enter the "now" has much to do with where you have been. The monologue cannot just start arbitrarily floating in space. It has a life of its own but it is still connected to the universe in its entirety.

What if you have no idea of the moment before? How do you play that question in your character's mind? It's as if Hamlet says to himself "What is to become of all this?" and after thought, his line is then an answer: "To be or not to be: that is the question." The first line of the monologue then springs off of the question rather than serves as a beginning all on its own.

Why is this important? In a monologue, the audience does not have the benefit of the through line of the play. All they have is a compartmentalized section of the writing and the character's thoughts. Therefor, the actor must create a frame in which the presentation must be made. Within this frame, the actor then can convey the thoughts of the character as they would appear in the full presentation of the work.

Playing the moment before the lights go up or the camera rolls then allows the audience to catch your character in the midst of their existence living their life in its entirety.

#4   PLAYING NOW
Creating Specific Objectives and reacting to stimuli
What is your main objective? Once you've determined what your character wants within the body of the monologue. Start to map it out within the context of the play or movie as a whole and within the section of the monologue.

THIS IS IMPORTANT TO REMEMBER. Characters don't always say or do what they want. Sometimes they say the opposite.

For example in Shakespeare's Julius Caesar, Caesar denies accepting the crown. But each time, he denies it with a little less enthusiasm.

CASCA: Why, there was a crown offered him: and being offered him, he put it by with the back of his hand, thus; and then the people fell a-shouting

BRUTUS: What was the second noise for?

CASCA: Why, for that too.

CASSIUS: They shouted thrice: what was the last cry for?

CASCA: Why, for that too.

BRUTUS: Was the crown offered him thrice?

CASCA: Ay, marry, was't, and he put it by thrice, everytime gentler than other, and at every putting-bymine honest neighbours shouted.

It is clear to the audience that Caesar covets the crown, but not all of his actions within the play reveal this. How would an actor break down this simple action into specific SUB BEATS which collectively support his/her major objective? Using the Julius Caesar example, each time the crown would be offered would be considered a specific beat. Broken down as follows:

Beat #1 First Crown offer: Quickly push away

Beat #2 Second Crown offer: Allow the crowd to cheer, the push away a little more slowly and a little less farther away.

Beat #3 Third Crown Offer: Allow the crowd to cheer and with great reluctance, push the crown slowly and with great effort away.

Each small beat, supports the major objective within this scene which is that Caesar wants nothing more than accept the crown.

Confronting Obstacles and reacting to stimuli

Obstacles to a character's objective can be both internal (such as self imposed fear, overbearing pride, lust for power) or external such as an adversary in the form of a person, place or thing.

Internal obstacle

In the case of Julius Caesar, an implied obstacle can be interpreted as internal. Caesar struggles with his own internal lust for power. He must fight his inner urge to just grab up the crown or even crown himself. Instead, he must struggle with his demon and appear to be humble and undeserving of such an honor. However, he eventually accepts the crown, but only with the overwhelming urging of the Roman citizenry.

External obstacle:
An external obstacle in this case could be Caesar's awareness of the political forces at hand. His quest for power must be supported by the citizens of Rome, the Army and the Senates. He would have to carefully align all of these forces and with their combined power take the throne. Once this fragile alliance fails he is assassinated by his rivals.

#5: PLAYING THE MOMENT AFTER
Everybody likes to know where they've been and where they're going
Your monologue has been spoken. Now what? What has happened during this journey? Has your character changed at all after all that has been said? If your character has spoken out loud to themselves, another character or the audience, has this auditory expression of their inner thoughts changed them in anyway? The answer to all of these questions is yes. And if it is yes the universe has changed as well as a result of the words being spoken. It may be a minute change, but it is a change nonetheless.

What happens next? You as the performer and your character have to answer the question: How has the universe changed and because of that change what will happen next. You don't have to write new lines to your monologue but there has to be a sense that something will follow.

How do you play this? We've come full circle. Your character must have some resolve intellectually, emotionally and physically.

How do you show this? The way your character contemplates on what he/she has just said in the monologue, or how the react emotionally, or how they physicalize the change. Your monologue doesn't end when the character utters the last line. It ends when the audience experiences the character's reaction to the last line. They want a sense of the effect of what has transpired and glimpse of what will be. That's what keeps them invested in your character, they want to know what's going to happen next.

When Macbeth speaks the last few lines of his soliloquy, the audience has had a glimpse of his tormented soul and has seen the shadow of the murder that is to come.

Macbeth
I have no spur To prick the sides of my intent,
but only Vaulting ambition,
which o'erleaps itself And falls on the other

When Macbeth utters the last line "And falls on the other," the moment after we see the murder in his eyes or a subtle shift in the way he walks off the stage.

SOME FINAL WORDS OF ADVICE

This is the part of the book where I get rattle off a few words which sound very cliché.

#1: Create the soufflé - Don't just read the recipe

Don't think about your monologue in terms of what you say but rather how you say it and what it means to your character and the audience. It's not just a list of words put together for amusement or recitation. The words, once spoken aloud become something else. For example if you were reciting the ingredients of a recipe for a soufflé, it's not enough to just say the words add two cups of flour, crack one egg etc. Your challenge is to take those words and create the soufflé. Not just any soufflé, your soufflé as it exists in the minds and hearts of your character and audience at that particular moment in time within the universe.

#2: Create the box

It's not enough to just create a character. As an actor, you must also be a producer and consider the way the character choices you have made will be presented. It's all about the show. Create the structure of the dynamic. That's the box. Go crazy inside the box you have created, if it falls apart build it up again. If you don't, you leave your opportunity of success to chance. Creative freedom is at its strongest when it is within a given structural dynamic.

#3   Don't forget Virtuosity

Why do we love the work of certain actors? Because, no matter what they do, they do it with such skill and style and think of choices that no one else could ever imagine. Think of Johnny Depp's creation of Captain Jack Sparrow in Pirates of the Caribbean or Marlon Brando's Godfather, Kate Blanchet's Elizabeth or Katherine Hepburn in the Aviator or Anthony Hopkin's Hannibal Lecter.   In each case, it was the actor that exercised the imagination, technical skill and sense of style to create an unforgettable character

#4.   Always find love in love in what you do

Try to connect to some sort of passion that you have always had about the creation of an imaginary characters living in an imaginary world. If it just becomes work, don't do it

#5.   Never get comfortable

Always question what appears to be the truth. You might be on the right road if you feel uneasy about what you are doing and that you might reveal too much. The excitement of the exploration and discovery will be felt by the viewers too.

#6.   Don't forget the basics

Aristotle stated: All human actions have one or more of these seven causes: chance, nature, compulsions, habit, reason, passion, desire. If you consider these in your creation of a character, you will not go wrong.

The Monologues

52 TWO PICK UP - PROLOGUE

(ENTER SHUFFLING CARDS)

Ever hear of the card game fifty two pick up? You probably know it as a practical joke... pretending to be a card game. Someone walks up to you and says... Wanna play fifty two pick up? You say... Sure! Then they throw the entire deck of cards onto the floor and tell you... Okay... pick em up!

Now, your part of the game... is to pick up all of the cards... and that's the end of the game. (BEAT) Not much fun... eh?

(BEAT)

Well it all depends on how you play...

(EXIT)

#1 YOU'RE IMPROVING (FEMALE)

(FOLDING A WAITERS APRON)

1. I'm home!
2. Hi. Sorry didn't mean so say I'm home so loud. I just
3. wanted to make sure you knew I was back. I always come
4. back. You can count on that.

(Beat)

5. Looks like I woke you up. I'm really sorry about that. But
6. it's nice to have someone to talk to when I get home. You
7. can understand that? Please don't think I'm complaining.
8. I'm not. In fact, I have always been a believer that the
9. universe, if you look at it in its entirety is made up of
10. more positive molecules than negative molecules. So, if
11. you just let the universe takes it's course, the best possible
12. scenario will always prevail. Even if you don't think it's the
13. best at the time, eventually you see the light. Take you
14. for instance.

(Beat)

15. You're improving. At least on the surface anyway. It's a
16. good start and tells me you are listening. Last night. When
17. I came home from work you actually got up out of bed and
18. said hello and you're here again tonight. You don't know
19. how nice that is after I've been on my feet for ten hours
20. waiting on tables. You have any idea how hard that is?
21. The first hour or so it's okay but then after that, it starts in
22. your ankles and then works its way up your calves to your
23. lower back. And that's where the pain stays right there. I
24. try to find things to lean on but that's not easy. Especially

25. tonight, I pulled counter. It's faster but the tips are bad.
26. Lots of dimes and quarters not much green. I know you
27. get annoyed when I come home and pour the change out
28. of my apron onto the kitchen table. You hate that sound.
29. I hate it too but I can't sleep until it's all counted. I like
30. to know where I stand as soon as possible. Good, bad or
31. indifferent, the facts are the facts and they never lie to you.
32. I'm right about that one because I know from experience.
33. I couldn't imagine trying to sleep without knowing where
34. I stood. If I didn't, I'd be counting in my sleep! Certain
35. things are important to know. Like you knowing I will
36. always come back when I leave and I knowing you'll always
37. be home when I return. Life is a journey and that's what
38. we're on you and me and the significant part of it is that
39. we are making the journey together. Right?

(Beat)

40. Right. You hungry? Look what I brought home for you.
41. Your favorite. Chicken

(Pulls a wrapped foil from her apron, opens it and places
it on the floor)

42. You have your snack while I count. And I won't throw the
43. change on the table. I'll be as quiet as I can.

#2 CONSERVATION (MALE)

(Holding a paper coffee cup)

1. I like to think of myself as a good person. I do good things
2. not bad things. Besides, when you do something that's
3. bad you somehow always get caught and have to pay the
4. price. Take conservation... now that's good and wasting is
5. bad. I try to save everything. You never know when you're
6. going to be needing this or that and it's nice to know that
7. it's there. Take this paper cup. I bought a cup of coffee
8. this morning. Paid over a dollar and half and didn't even
9. use cream. Drank the coffee.

10. Which by the way was either bitter or burnt. Had a sharp
11. almost metallic taste to it.

(Hold the cup upside down)

12. Now what? The coffee is gone and all I'm left with is this
13. paper compressed twelve-ounce coffee cup. What does it
14. say to me?

(Puts it to his ear and whispering in an English accent, the
voice of the cup.)

15. "Hold on to me ... don't throw me away. I can serve
16. you further. You can learn from me." And I thought to
17. myself, what can I possibly learn from an empty twelve
18. ounce paper coffee cup? And before I could toss it, the
19. cup whispered to me again.

20. "Put me to your ear and listen." So I thought... what have
21. I got to lose? So I put the cup to my ear and listened.

22. Then the cup spoke again. "What do you hear?" I said
23. nothing...

24. Listen more closely I did... and then echoing faintly at
25. first then louder. I began to hear a slow and deliberate
26. chant. It said ... "Be bad... get away with it" ... Really?
27. Be bad? How? Like rob a bank? Do you want me to rob
28. a bank? Is that it? Cheat on my girlfriend. I don't have a
29. girlfriend? I listened again. "Be bad... get away with it."
30. Bad? Should I steal something? And if I can get away with
31. it, I want it to be something really good like a Porsche. A
32. hot red convertible Porche... *mucho caliente!* What am I
33. saying? I can't do that. I just can't be bad... it's not in me.

(To cup)

34. I just can't be bad. I just can't. I'm afraid to be bad. I'm
35. afraid of what will happen. What do you say to that?

(Put cup to ear)

36. But this time nothing. I closed my eyes and concentrated
37. as hard as I could but still nothing. I put my mouth
38. over the cup and whispered. Hello! Hello, are you still
39. with me...?

40. Hello... Nothing. Not a sound. It was as if whatever life
41. it had was all consumed all in that one moment and one
42. message ... then gone. Then I thought to myself Be Bad...
43. Get away with it... Be bad... be bad ...

(Beat, a long look at the cup, then crumple it in one hand. A quick look over each shoulder, then throw it to the ground and exit.)

#3 STUFF OF LIFE (MALE)

1. It's the weekend! Woke up this morning around 6:00 A.M.
2. to the sound of birds chirping and flapping around my
3. window. Let me say it again... it's the weekend, so I don't
4. have to get up early! But I still do because I want to get
5. out as much of the day as possible... and like most days, I
6. start out with unbridled optimism. Right before my eyes
7. I see a new day, like a blank page with nothing on it but
8. the possibility of wonderful things.

(Beat)

9. Then, I get out of bed and it's all down hill from there. As
10. soon as you put your two feet on the ground, it hits you
11. right between the eyes like the headlight of an oncoming
12. freight train. It's what I call the stuff of life. You know all
13. the crap you *have* to do that keeps you from doing the
14. things you dream of doing.

(Stretching with a yawn)

15. Here I am out of bed with the sun shining on me. What
16. adventure will I embark on? Got to do the laundry. If I
17. don't, I'll have to were the same underwear that I did
18. yesterday. I can deal with that but I can't wear that same
19. blue shirt I've been wearing all week. I can't wear it again.
20. I just can't... unless I can get that tomato sauce stain off of
21. the sleeve. I should have used a napkin... then I wouldn't
22. be in this situation.

(Beat)

23. You know, the stain is really not that noticeable … I think
24. I roll up the sleeve and stretch one more wearing out of it
25. and the underwear. What the hell... Problem solved, now
26. on with the adventure! Right? Not a chance. I'm hungry.
27. I haven't eaten anything for at least eight hours. Nothing
28. in the fridge except a half empty carton of milk and some
29. fruit loops. I'll just have a quick bowl of cereal. Wait, can't
30. do that... don't know how long that milk has been in the
31. fridge... and there's no way I'm going to stick my nose
32. through the top of the carton to see if it's sour. Cause
33. if it is … sour, I don't want those sour milk molecules
34. mixing with my I haven't eaten anything since last night
35. molecules. That could be very messy. Screw it.

36. I'll eat out. I'll go have coffee and a scone. Very continental
37. breakfast. Okay, let's do it! Wait... can't eat out. No cash.
38. I used it all up on the cash only line at the supermarket
39. last night when I bought that bag of pretzels. You can't
40. go on an adventure without cash. Got to go to the bank.
41. But it's the weekend, the banks are closed. No, that's not
42. right... they're open. In fact everything is open. So I'll
43. make a quick stop at the ready teller before I begin my
44. adventure... and since I'm there I should probably drop
45. off my dress pants at the cleaners, and right around the
46. corner from there is the post office. Got to return that
47. exercise DVD I bought, but wait... I need to pick up a
48. packing box and some tape. I can go to the stationary
49. store for that. That's right next to the pet store. I need to
50. pick up some of that special diet dry food for Buddy …
51. that's my dog. He can't eat regular dry food. Can't digest
52. it... gets very flatulent. So it's the special low gravel diet
53. for him. Better for all of us. Where is Buddy?

(Beat)

54. Still asleep. Can't blame him. It's the weekend. (Whisper)
55. Okay, let's do it! I'm off on life's adventure! (Searching)
56. Now, if I could only find my car keys.

#4 SPACE #1 (FEMALE)

(Holding a yellow legal pad)

1.   ... And here is the main room. Actually, the only room.
2.   This space is well appointed with the walls and a single
3.   multi lock one hundred percent metal front door entry
4.   way which spills graciously into the outside hallway which
5.   is adorned in Spanish antique Rosewood red spray paint
6.   calligraphy *Jose es un bendeho and Maria e puta*. All in
7.   perfect visual counterpoint to the laminate vinyl tile
8.   flooring with belvedere asbestos trim. Despite the implied
9.   grandeur, this space never gives up its homey feel. If you
10.   look out this half window just slightly left of the satellite
11.   dish you can fully enjoy the sweeping views to the north,
12.   west and if you stand tip toe, to the south as far as the
13.   eye can see. Well as far as that grey billboard. This space
14.   is particularly unique because it brilliantly combines
15.   two apartments to create one stunning 400-square-foot
16.   home. As you can see, no detail has been spared from
17.   engineered flooring (actually plywood) and single room
18.   modular design featuring and exclusive master bathroom
19.   bedroom combination space offering you the opportunity
20.   to sleep and wash simultaneously... and did I mention the
21.   combo closet, shower deep soaking tub. The green subway
22.   restroom tiles were kept original to give the room a true
23.   retro feel. This well designed single room layout doesn't
24.   have the cumbersome features most 3 bedrooms multi-
25.   bath spaces contain. This is space is a true minimalist
26.   paradise. You are not encumbered with a spacious living
27.   room, full dining room, open kitchen with informal bar,
28.   laundry room, plus a den that can be converted to a fourth
29.   bedroom. This space literally propels you out the door and
30.   down the specially designed freight elevator to enjoy the

31. city and all it has to offer. You'll enjoy going out every day
32. to a public restrooms, restaurants, the gym, steam rooms,
33. the library. Just think of all the new friends and business
34. contacts you will meet and you can do it all without the
35. hassle of clean up afterwards. This is true freedom at its
36. best. That what makes this space a true charmer at one
37. point eight.

(Beat)

38. Between you and me, there's a little wiggle room on that
39. number. But not much. Just think of it this way. If you
40. lived here ... you'd be home now. No traffic jams or long
41. train rides back to the suburbs. You'd be sitting pretty
42. in the city... like a bug in a rug ... in the warm glow of
43. firelight. Well, actually, the amber blue glow of the pilot
44. light in the gas kitchen cook top fireplace combo unit.
45. Definitely a space you can call home.

#5 SPACE 2 (FEMALE)

(Holding a fancy file folder)

1. Before we go in, I wanted to give you a bit a background
2. information about the **space** you are about to see. This is
3. a prime location and one of those addresses in Manhattan
4. that everyone is talking about. It has been featured in
5. many major newspapers and magazines over the last year.
6. The market value on this exclusive space can only rise
7. with the passage of time. The adjoining tower is a full
8. service hotel where you as an owner can at additional cost
9. utilize the multitude of the five star services that such an
10. establishment normally offers its guests. The concierge
11. is available to you twenty four hours a day, seven days a
12. week. In addition, you have available to you the full range
13. of amenities offered in your own tower including tennis
14. courts, lap pool and spa located on the roof level. Any
15. questions before we go in?

(Beat)

16. Before we enter, there is just one thing I want to mention
17. which probably needs to be explained. Last year. I think
18. it was last year. Well almost a year ago there was a slight
19. mishap sort of a "Alusus naturae" ... Nothing that hasn't
20. happened before in a city of this size. Just an accident of
21. sorts. Well actually not an accident in the true sense of the
22. word. More accurately a murder. Now, don't be alarmed. It
23. didn't involve illegal drugs or fire arms. Nothing like that.
24. What happened here was a crime of passion where one
25. party in a moment of pure rage took the life of another.
26. This was not really a criminal act but an act made in the
27. absence of reason. And as I said earlier no actual weapons

28. were used nor was there any premeditation involved. This
29. was just what can I say a simple disagreement between a
30. husband and wife that took a bad turn. There was a third
31. party involved. However, the lover in question was mere
32. standby and the fact that he died of multiple stab wounds
33. had no direct correlation to the anger and physical harm
34. inflicted by each spouse upon one another. The murder
35. suicide aspect of this event was never clearly established.
36. It was however, inferred quiet effectively along with
37. the satanic ritual angle in the tabloid press here in the
38. city. The fact that you are from *out of the area* would not
39. necessarily mean you hadn't seen it on television or read
40. it in the news. I assume that Nepal gets the major outlets
41. ... CNN and FOX NEWS. Such stories have a way of
42. titillating the public and once it is known that you are the
43. new occupants, you might be sought out by a member of
44. the press, a parapsychologist or perhaps a Satanic cultist.
45. Inquiring minds will want to know how it is to live in such
46. a space knowing what had occurred here? But in reality...
47. a space is just a space... air and four walls. Personally, I
48. don't think the whole karma theory holds any water. Well,
49. I did want to just mention it in passing before we go in.

(Beat, enter space)

50. Now then, finally the space... isn't it magnificent? This is
51. the main room ideal for entertaining. Well appointed with
52. the crown gargoyle moldings throughout. The Crimson
53. Red Carrara marble entry way literally spills on to the
54. darkened rust rosewood flooring with black granite trim
55. highlighted with a speckled blood rust sprinkle detail.
56. The stark stone alter centerpiece has been given a splash
57. of color with the insertion of travertine hand-crafted
58. Celtic symbols stained in a dark Al'orange mist. Despite

59. the implied grandeur, this space in its own way attempts
60. to decompose the formality of its design in favor of an
61. almost rustic lived in feeling. (Beat) If you look over to
62. your left, you will notice the exquisite view of the river
63. and on the opposite window a splendid view of Central
64. Park. Truly a view to die for.

(Beat)

65. Now, if I may, onto the bedrooms and bath.

#6 BAD SIDE (MALE)

(Singing Woodstock)

1. I came upon a child a God... he was walking along the
2. road ... You like that song? It's Crosby Stills and Nash,
3. from the sixties. Or are you a seventies type? Do a little
4. dance... Make a little love... get down tonight ... Come
5. on... don't be mad at me... I didn't mean to go off on you.
6. It's just my personality ... sometimes I go off. It's like a
7. little red button in my brain that gets pressed and boom!
8. The beast is released.

(Singing)

9. I'm sorry... so sorry... please accept my apology...

(No reply)

10. Come on... throw me a bone here.
11. I'm trying to make this work.

(Beat, a bit irritated)

12. So, do you really think I have a bad side? Well it's about
13. time you found out. I don't take crap from anyone...
14. and that includes you. We've been going out for what?
15. five months now and you finally have gotten around to
16. telling me this? I should be angry but I'm not. And that's
17. because I agree with you completely. Like the other night
18. when you wanted Chinese and I wanted Italian. What did
19. we eat?

(Beat)

20. Italian... otherwise it would be ciao baby. That's the bad
21. side talking.

22. But I do care about what **you** think and feel. It's just that
23. I'm the kind of person that likes to express what **they** feel.
24. I don't think there's anything wrong with that. And... I
25. want you to know that there's a good side to by bad side.
26. The good side is that I am totally committed to everything
27. I believe in. I don't mince around. I am totally committed
28. to you!

29. See, now you know where we stand. And another good
30. thing is that I like you just the way you are. I'm not going
31. to try to change you into something else that fits **my** needs.
32. You can be who you want to be and I'll be who I want to
33. be... and that will be that.

(Beat)

34. There is one thing. Just one thing. I don't like to walk
35. and *you do.* If I had it my way, I'd take a cab around the
36. corner. In fact, if I ever became very wealthy... you know
37. hit the lottery or something, I wouldn't go out and buy a
38. forty-room mansion with a view of the river. No... the first
39. thing I'd do is get myself a personal chauffeur to drive me
40. everywhere I'd want to go. I'd get a very stacked limo with
41. a television, bar and seats that massage you while you sit
42. in them. Now that's entertainment for me. Being driven
43. around. And for you it's walking? I just don't understand
44. what that's about? What's the walking thing do for you?
45. You get to put one foot in front of the other. You mess
46. up your shoes, and you get to smell cigarettes and cheap
47. perfume. Not much fun.

(Beat)

48. You hungry? Let's get something to eat... Italian. And let's
49. take a cab okay?

(Beat)

50. You got a problem with that?

#7 CRIME (MALE)

(At podium)

1. I want to thank you all for allowing me to talk to you today.
2. Especially today. Your graduation day. Graduation from
3. high school... A journey which began some twelve years
4. ago and maybe for more than a few, a little longer. But
5. it doesn't matter how long it took to get you here. The
6. point is that you **are** here and you're about to embark on
7. a new journey. One that will take you to many places.

(Beat)

8. Guess the point is that today. Especially today the air is
9. filled with possibilities of *what can be*. What *should* be. All
10. those things we wonder about when we look up at the sky
11. at night and wonder where do I fit in to this universe?
12. What will I become? And you ask yourself that question
13. over and over again. And the answer sometimes comes to
14. you and just as you think you've got it all figured out. It
15. changes. And that's all part of the fun of it isn't. That it
16. changes. You think you want to be a lawyer then a rock star,
17. then a veterinarian. And that's the way it's supposed to be.

(BEAT)

18. That's what is a **normal life**. And if that's abruptly taken
19. away from you... that's a crime. I mean we all have to
20. die someday... but we really don't think much about it
21. because we figure it won't happen for a long while and
22. probably when it does, we'll be so old we won't even know
23. or care anymore. But the crime I'm talking about is when
24. it comes too soon. Untimely and uninvited like a bullet in

25. your head. Boom! Then black. Now I'm not talking about
26. just and end to an idea. I'm talking about an ending
27. with no reprieve. The final end. The Blackness of black.
28. Complete. That's it. Done.

(Beat)

29. Now you all know who I am and you knew my kid brother
30. Johnny. He was my shadow always three feet behind me
31. wondering what I was going to do next and if he could do
32. it too. At the time, if you asked me, I would have told you
33. that this kid follows me like a puppy dog... I can't stand it.
34. I need space. I would give anything to have him standing
35. behind me today. Right up behind me close saying what
36. are we going to do now Chance? He called me Chance
37. because I always like to leave everything to chance. Never
38. planned a thing. I went to this school and I sat in those
39. bleachers on a hot June day just like you are right now. I
40. sat out there while someone came up to this podium and
41. spoke. It was awhile ago. I admit that. But it wasn't so long
42. ago that I can't remember what it was like. I sat out there,
43. just like you are now and listened to someone come up
44. here and speak about tomorrow and I thought... What a
45. crock of shit. Let's get on with it. I can't wait to bust out of
46. this rat hole... Yeah, let's put the pedal to the metal and
47. get on with it. The sun is beating down on my head and
48. this stupid cap and gown are making me sweat like an
49. animal.

(Beat)

50. I hear a couple of you laughing at that. Cause you know
51. I'm right. And I won't take up much more of your time.
52. Mr. Carter your principal was nice enough to let me talk

53. to you today and I thank him for that. I wanted to talk to
54. all of you at one time. Johnny might have been sitting out
55. there with you all today. But he's not here... and a lot of
56. you probably want me to say he's still with us in spirit...
57. but really **that** would be bull shit. Johnny's not here at
58. all. He's gone. And you all know how and why that is the
59. case. Johnny was shot in the head... right across the street
60. there. He came back to school at night to get his physics
61. book out of his locker. He had a test the next morning
62. and waited until the last minute to study. Just like me.
63. Who the hell ever uses physics anyway...?

64. Shot in the head. And maybe shot by someone sitting out
65. there today. And why? No special reason... just because he
66. was there. Police said it was gang related. You don't need
67. a text book to tell you that. Sure there's gangs. Always
68. have been groups of people getting into it with other
69. groups of people. That's nothing new. But what they're
70. not telling you is you throw 3700 kids in a school that's
71. designed to hold maybe 2400 and you know all you need
72. to know about a bullet in the head. Johnny was just at
73. the wrong place at the wrong time. He took a chance and
74. lost. I might have done the same thing. He took a chance
75. and lost it all.

(Beat)

76. The reason why I came here is to talk about tomorrow. I
77. see you sitting here today all pumped up about getting out
78. of here and making some wild ass future for yourself. And
79. that's great! That's the way it should be! When you get
80. out there, the world is going to be wonderful adventure
81. and it's going to be a pain in the ass too. It's also going
82. to be harsh and cold and too expensive, too crowded and

83. sometimes you will want to chuck it all. But you won't...
84. that would be a crime. Instead, you'll deal with it calmly
85. and make the world better placc. I want you all to promise
86. me that ... make the world a better place ... Not just the
87. words. I want you *really* to do it... or that would really be
88. a crime. Do it for yourself

(Beat)

89. And do it for Johnny.
(EXIT)

#8 MEMORY, PAIN AND TRUTH

(FEMALE)

1. Now that I'm older and I don't mean old like I'm ready
2. to pack it in. I mean older than I was before... older than
3. I have been and now have a better understanding of
4. things than when I was a child. The funny thing about
5. your memory is that your brain is like computer hardware
6. and all of the neurons and ganglia are software. You get
7. the basic version when you're born and then as time goes
8. by you get automatically upgraded to the current version.
9. Here's what I mean. When you think back to a significant
10. event in your past, you're looking at it from now. You see it
11. through the eyes of all the new upgrades you have picked
12. up along the way. So things that made you extremely
13. happy like getting ready for Santa Clause on Christmas
14. Eve, now when reflected on is somehow not the same.
15. That experience of wonder has been upgraded and what
16. was a joy-filled event has been added to with experiences
17. like waiting on long lines at the mall, driving in holiday
18. traffic and seeing Christmas decorations go up in October.
19. All the new information happened between then and now.
20. And even now is changing as I speak to you.

(Beat, waiting.)

21. You've just been upgraded... just now. Doesn't feel any
22. different does it? But trust me it is. You've changed and
23. you don't even know it. Let's call it the "now rule". And
24. like all rules... there's an exception to the "now rule" That
25. has to do with extreme pain or fear. If something scared
26. the crap out of you as a kid, you probably are still afraid of
27. it now. Only difference is that you won't admit it. Now for

28. me, it's always been spiders. Isn't there a word for that?
29. Arachnophobia. Means abnormal fear of spiders. When I
30. was a child, I'd step on the little bastards any time I saw one.
31. I hated them so much I'd cross the street in the middle to
32. step on one. What about spiders now? I still fear and hate
33. them... the only difference is now I can't show it the same
34. way. I can't scream, jump up and down and shout SPIDER!
35. I'm older and have been upgraded... can't do that. Now,
36. I've got to be cool and say check out that spider ... he's
37. bigger than a Toyota... better get him before he moves in
38. with his family. Then quickly, stomp him. The same goes
39. for pain. You hit your finger with a hammer and it hurts
40. so much you think you're going to explode. If you were
41. a child you'd scream I want my mommy! Can't do that
42. now, you've been upgraded. Now, what you do is say? I'm
43. bleeding through the black and blue... but I'm okay. Let's
44. go to the mall.And you're thinking to yourself... If I die
45. at least I'll be hanging out at the mall... that's a great way
46. to go.There's also emotional pain... fear of death, or the
47. unknown... something like walking into a dark room. Now
48. when I was a child... I just wouldn't go into a dark room.
49. No way no how. I just couldn't walk into the darkness not
50. knowing what was in the same space as me ... the boogie
51. man or even worse my older brother. It was a deep-rooted
52. fear which came from my basic instinct for self survival.
53. And now... I've been upgraded... I still won't walk into
54. a dark room. No way, no how. There still is no way I'm
55. walking into the darkness without knowing what I might
56. walk into. A pole, a wall and how embarrassing would that
57. be. You're at work and they ask... where'd you get that
58. bruise across your face? You can never say... I walked into a
59. wall. Upgrading forces you to create an alternate image...
60. I was mugged. Hit across the face with a baseball bat... but
61. I fought them off and took the bat away. Actually, I kicked

62. their ass. That's the kind of woman I am. They look at
63. you in silence for a moment then say: cool... I wish I was
64. mugged and did that...Instantly you're their hero instead
65. of someone afraid of the boogie man. Not bad eh?

(Beat)

66. So where's the truth in all this? We come down to
67. the ultimate question. What is real to you? Have your
68. memories and pain been totally negated by upgrading?
69. Has the original you been upgraded out of existence?
70. Don't think so. Nothing ever really gets erased... just
71. upgraded. You're still in there Somewhere in that dark
72. room with the lights turned off.

(Beat, then exit.)

#9 FROM THE EDGE (FEMALE)

(Enter with a flair wearing a French beret)

1. Whatever you do, don't tell anyone about this. I mean
2. no one! If you do, I will never speak to you again.
3. You promise?

(Beat)

4. Okay, so, the other day I finally got my ass in gear and went
5. walking across town and got lost. I figured how can you be
6. in Paris and not walk around right? So I went out the front
7. door of my hotel and right there, I'm in trouble. There's
8. this door man or bell hop or whatever who always smiles
9. at me. I think his name is Charles. So, I'm walking out
10. the door trying to remember which way was which when
11. there's Charles standing at the front doorway smiling at
12. me. I smiled back and went out into the street but really
13. didn't know where I was going.

(Beat)

14. There was no way. I was going to ask Charles where to
15. go. He might get the wrong idea. So there I was walking
16. down a dark street in the city of lights. It was so cold out
17. and I was thinking to myself how do these people do it,
18. because here the town is so small that everyone walks,
19. but it's so freaking cold. I walked up for a few blocks
20. and there wasn't anything opened. Maybe I made a right
21. maybe a left. I was just trying to find some light and some
22. people. But it seemed everywhere I turned it was getting
23. darker! I finally found a phone and called this guy I met
24. at the train station the day before. No answer! What the
25. Fo! Don't these people ever stay home?! I finally reached

26. this little corner café. There was a waiter cleaning off a
27. table and I asked if he knew where I was. I asked him in
28. English rather than French. I just couldn't get my brain
29. to work in the cold. I wanted to say it French but then
30. I just really couldn't conjugate the verb where I am. I
31. remember saying to myself screw it just say it in English.
32. I did. The waiter smiled and pointed (without speaking)
33. to a cobble stone street. Go figure? Not even a word. I
34. figured what the hell? I deserve what I get for traveling
35. alone. So I walked up the street and saw light and people!
36. There were lots of little cars, mushed looking runabouts
37. wearing scarves and sweaters and bicycles. It was extremely
38. noisy and that made me extremely happy then sad again.
39. Suddenly a little voice spoke to me and said. You're
40. hungry... I wanted to eat. But then I got sad because eating
41. is such a social thing and I just hate to eat alone. Eating
42. alone is for losers. I thought this to myself as I stopped to
43. get a croissant. The old man at the counter smiled at me
44. like he knew me. But he didn't. But the smile made me
45. feel at home and all at once I said thank you... but not in
46. English. In French! It just poured out of me like a song.
47. Merci... Merci! He said thank you back every time I said
48. it which must have been at least twenty times. I washed
49. the croissant down with the lightest and most beautiful
50. cup of coffee I have ever had in my life. As I walked away
51. from this magical café the entire world seemed to open
52. up before my eyes. I turned the darkened corner onto
53. the main boulevard and there it was... the Eiffel Tower
54. glowing like a jewel in the night. I found myself walking
55. toward it and realized that the weather is only bad if
56. you think about it, so I kept walking and put a smile on
57. my face and walked some more and before I knew it... I
58. found myself standing in front of Charles and my hotel.
59. I thought to myself finally made it home! I love Paris!
(EXIT WITH A FLARE)

#10 ROPE (MALE)

(Holding a section of rope then sit for a moment, then...)

1. Just picked up this piece of rope up outside on the way
2. in here. It was just sitting on the floor. All by itself with
3. no other pieces of rope around. Somebody probably
4. cut it off a much longer piece, used it for something and
5. then tossed it away. Can you guess how long this piece of
6. rope is? What do you think? Maybe about a foot... foot
7. and half long? But that's not the way it begun. This piece
8. here, probably started out as a single strand of twine tied
9. together over and over again, until it became larger and
10. larger... probably ended up about three hundred yards
11. long. Then, little by little it was cut away over and over
12. again until this severed piece found its way onto the floor.
13. Doesn't look like it can be used for much now. Too short
14. and too old to do anyone much good. But I thought I'd
15. bring it with me and give it a proper finish rather than
16. just let it sit there on the ground. (Hold rope reverently)
17. Here goes. "Rope" Thank you. You've always held a knot
18. well. Didn't stretch too much. Strong and always there
19. to tie things to the ground so they wouldn't blow away in
20. the wind. You held everything in place when we couldn't
21. and taught us we could work together. You served your
22. purpose well. And now, all that's left is this small piece.
23. No one wants to be like a piece of rope.

(Beat)

24. No one.

(Places the rope down gently, takes one last look and exits.)

#11 STARLET O'HARA (FEMALE)

(Sitting blandly slumped forward with sun glasses on to a camera person we don't see.)

1. Are we on yet? No? (Beat)
2. Yes?
3. Will somebody throw me a bone here?
4. Now?
5. Not yet.
6. Yes?
7. Yes.

(Springs to life with a smile.)

8. G W T W... no. Okay, it's true! I didn't think anybody knew
9. it... we've been talking first generally then more specifically
10. on and off for about a year now. You know... mostly social
11. chat at parties... openings or clubs... and also about the
12. possibility of working together on a project. And then,
13. maybe a month ago my theatrical agent Darla signed up
14. with the same personal trainer as Steven. So she kept
15. seeing him at the gym, then ran into him again walking
16. on Broad Beach in Malibu. I guess, the planets were lined
17. and the energy of the universe wanted this to happen. I
18. was sitting, I think it was Starbucks or shopping on Sunset
19. Plaza when I got the call, that they wanted me to look at
20. the script. It was so amazing because I've been a big fan
21. of the original G W T W for months. I wanted to read
22. the original book but then changed my mind. I didn't
23. want it to influence in any way the images I have always
24. cherished from the original film which I saw as a child on
25. TV. Steven said he liked my work in The Fish Hooker and

26. wanted to expand the original role of the heroine Scarlet
27. O'Hara just for me. But you know how the big studios are.
28. They, at first, didn't think I could carry the picture. They
29. wanted a bigger name, more box office boffo Let's face
30. it, making movies is a business. A cold-hearted business.
31. You're only as good as your last project's box office gross.
32. I think Steven really pushed for me and the studio agreed
33. to let me do screen test. When I got there, I thought
34. they would put me on a mansion porch, in a beautiful
35. white crinoline gown with ruffles but instead they had
36. me wear this really skimpy tropical top and wanted me
37. to bite a dirty radish and say the line I'll never be hungry
38. again... You know that part in the script when Scarlet has
39. the epiphany that she's going to survive and become rich
40. and famous. I thought to myself... all those acting classes,
41. studying Stanislovski then Meisner and here I am eating
42. dirt. It was actually stage dirt which won't really hurt you
43. if you eat it. But... it's still pretty creepy... eating dirt. But
44. I did it... and I did it with joy. Anything to get to work
45. with Steven.

(Beat)

46. And the best part of this is... I got the part! That's what I
47. love about this business. When it's good... it's great and
48. when it's bad, it really sucks... but getting this part and
49. being able to finally work with Steven is G R E A T. The
50. script is definitely updated, but I won't go into any details.
51. Don't want to give anything away... you'll just have to wait
52. until the movie comes out... even though the theatrical
53. debut is really just a trailer for the DVD release... so you'll
54. have to wait until then. (Laughs). I can tell you this. I
55. have a very nice opening scene... I think I can tell you that.
56. (Looks out beyond the camera) I can say that... can't I?

57. Okay... are you sure?

(Beat)

58. Okay. Here it is... I loved it so much I memorized it.

59. FADE IN: The sound of distant drums foretelling the
60. battle that is to come. Then endless conflict which tore a
61. fledgling nation apart. A conflict born of blood which pits
62. father again son, brother against brother, sister against
63. sister, mother against daughter, mother against father,
64. aunt against uncle, cousin against second cousin ... Let's
65. face it everybody's against everybody... it's the Civil War!

(Beat)

66. But really, is that cool or what? The script is pretty much
67. locked... and I've been working out with the personal
68. trainer that Hilary Swank used for Million Dollar Baby.
69. If I'm going to be jumping from a southern plantation
70. to war-torn Charleston... in some skimpy top... I want
71. to be B U F F.... baby. No fuzzy lense for me... just the
72. real thing.

(In Southern dialect)

73. *Fiddlee Dee... I just can't wait for tomorrow!*

(Holding big smile too long and then,)

74. That's not quite the right line is it? Did you say cut?

(Beat)

75. We're done? Okay. Great... couldn't wait to get off this
76. seat, something very sticky. I think I sat on some chewing
77. gum. Hope this is washable.

#12 GUYS LIKE STOOGES GIRLS LIKE LUCY (MALE)

1. I'm glad you came... sit down.

(Beat)

2. You're probably pissed at me for not calling you back.
3. You've called me what is it... seven or eight times... and
4. left messages. Maybe another seven or eight times that
5. were hang ups. I hate when people don't return my calls.
6. I really do... and you're probably thinking... that's what
7. guys do... you give them you're number and they don't
8. ever call you. That's not why I didn't call. I didn't call
9. because I didn't have anything to say. I mean I knew what
10. I was feeling but I didn't know how to verbalize it in a
11. way that would not hurt you. You've been hinting that
12. you and I could have a beautiful life together. And when
13. I didn't respond... you said... I think it was last week, that
14. the only way you would spend a lot of time with a person
15. is if you had a commitment. Remember that?

(Beat)

16. You said all that... and I didn't respond. Now, I can...
17. Guys... like Stooges and... girls like Lucy. I'm not trying
18. to be glib or anything like that. But really, it's the bottom
19. line. I know you want to go to the next step with this
20. relationship and... I would... if I could... but I can't. I just
21. can't... go to the next step or really any step.

(Beat)

22. You and I are friends... we started out that way and nothing
23. about that has changed. I really enjoy the times when we
24. are together. Last week when we went to the zoo was really
25. great. I haven't done anything like that in a long time. As
26. you know, I don't like when any animal is caged up... but
27. with you I got past that and had fun. The picnic in the
28. park was also very different for me. I always thought of
29. picnics as eating hot dogs, hamburgers things like that.
30. You took the whole picnic thing to a new level with the
31. table cloth, champagne and caviar. Now, that's something
32. I would have never done on my own without you. It was
33. great.

(Beat)

34. But here's the deal... I am not able to make a commitment
35. to you. It's not that I want to be with anybody else. I just
36. can't commit... to anything. I just want to take each day
37. as an adventure and see where it leads me. When we
38. first met, we exchanged stories of our past relationships.
39. And you know that in *my* case, it wasn't easy. I did the
40. commitment thing and where did it get me? It got me tied
41. down, in trench warfare ever damn day I was involved. I
42. just can't go back to *that* again. I'm not saying that you
43. are remotely anything like that, but it's just the idea of it
44. that I can't agree to. I can't tell you what or where I will
45. be tomorrow or the next day. I'm just not able to do that.
46. Since we've been seeing each other, we've never planned
47. a thing... we just are in the moment. At least that's where
48. I've been.

(Beat)

49. What do you think?

(Silence)

50. I'm not asking you to say anything. But I wanted to talk
51. to you face to face rather than on the phone. I think it's
52. better exchanging voice messages on our cell phones.
53. We will know exactly how I feel. No misinterpretation.

(Wait for a reply, there is none.)

54. Okay? Hopefully... no hard feelings between us.

(Beat, she's about to cry)

55. See, when your lip quivers like that? That's just like Lucy.
56. Every time she didn't get what she wanted, her lip would
57. quiver, she would cry and say... Ricky... and Ricky, the poor
58. bastard would always give in. It's just your way of trying to
59. control me! You probably don't even know you're doing
60. it. But it's not going to happen! Not this time!

61. Sorry you're crying, but its not going to work... YOU ARE
62. NOT GOING TO CONTROL ME... You are just going to
63. piss me off! So stop crying ...

(Beat)

64. I *am not* Ricky... I'm Moe... ... do you know what that
65. means? So stop crying!
(Beat)

66. I said, STOP CRYING!

(Ominously stand up.)

67. Ricky gives in... I don't. You know what Moe does to
68. Curly when he gets mad... DO YOU KNOW WHAT MOE
69. DOES?

(No reply. Rises with a clenched fist.)

70. HEY NUMB SKULL!

(Fist raised to hit. Then, drops fist and backs off Exits.)

#13 SUBSCRIPTIONS (FEMALE)

(Sitting holding a folded magazine - with artificial upper class British accent)

1. I have always thought of myself as a sophisticated person.
2. Always aware of current events, fashion... especially what's
3. in... and out. It doesn't come easy. I have to work hard at
4. it. It takes hours of concentration to get it all just right.
5. I consider every detail. My appearance, clothing, foods I
6. ingest and of course, the people I choose to share time
7. with. In each case, our associations with the outside
8. world become symbols which are used by other educated
9. individuals to determine who we are. In essence, modern
10. society is a composition of such symbols. The most common
11. are the car you drive, the restaurants you frequent,
12. your zip code and private school you attend. These are
13. the most rudimentary to reflect your social status, but
14. often overlooked is one image that can ruinous to you at
15. every level.

(Beat)

16. It's your magazine subscriptions. The magazines one
17. subscribes to say a lot about where you fit into society.
18. Are you on the top of the ladder or on one of the lower
19. rungs trying to climb up? No mincing around here...
20. subscriptions come to our homes with our names and
21. addresses embossed upon them. They are a literal
22. extension of who we are and have to be selected very
23. carefully. Not for the articles they contain but rather
24. for their name and appearance of their cover. When
25. you have guests, arrive at your home, you want to have
26. these periodicals strategically placed so they may be

27. seen. Subscriptions are your billboards to the world!
28. Saying this is who I am! Look at me! And just *who* are
29. you? Are you hip fashionable and part of the jet set?
30. Well, then you're a GQ or Vogue... or perhaps you are
31. serious minded, conservative, wealthy... your M O N E Y
32. or AMERICAN VENTURE. Are you a liberal left wing
33. east coast intellectual? Then your ATLANTIC REVIEW
34. or the NEW YORKER. How about a celebrity or industry
35. insider...? That's Daily Variety. So on and so forth...

(Beat)

36. The moment you flip open those pages or reveal the title
37. cover, the pictures and the words of your subscription
38. become an extension of you! Just think you and your
39. magazine together as one enormous allegory painting
40. your portrait for a world too busy to stop and look!

(Beat)

41. You know the old adage. It's a jungle out there... predators
42. and prey. Which one do you want to be?

(Beat, listening)

43. That's what I thought you'd say.

(Beat)

44. Shall we have our tea? Excellent...

(Places folded magazine under arm and exits.)

#14 TWO KINDS OF PEOPLE (FEMALE)

(Holding damp rag)

1. There are two kinds of people in the world. Those who
2. are *served* by others (The servees) and the rest of us who
3. do all the work... the servers. I am in the second group...
4. the servers. I spend all of my life in the service of others.
5. Throwing out the garbage, picking up socks and used
6. tissues, recycling the old newspapers, cleaning the crumbs
7. off of the kitchen table. This is **MY** life. I was put on this
8. earth to serve. Not to be served. I only wish that once in
9. my life there would be someone who would do something
10. for me. Worry about me. Think about me ... then I'd be
11 a servee... How wonderful.

(Beat)

12. Who the hell am I kidding?

(Throws the rag on her shoulder and exits)

#15 COLLEGE (MALE)

1. I never really thought about going to college until the day
2. I graduated from high school and kind of figured I'd have
3. to go somewhere... so I'd better apply. So I did, went to a
4. junior college, then a four-year school and then graduate
5. school. So, I guess you can say I went to college.

(Beat)

6. But, when I was a kid, all I ever wanted to do was play
7. with my toys and have fun. When adults would ask me
8. what I wanted to do when I grew up I'd always say that I
9. wanted to be a lawyer. I didn't really know what a lawyer
10. was but I knew it made my mother happy because she
11. would always say lawyers make a lot of money! So go to
12. college and be a lawyer... so you don't turn out like your
13. father. I never knew what that meant either. My father
14. seemed fine to me. I always wondered what she meant
15. when she said don't turn out to be like your father. What
16. I remember most about my father was that he worked a
17. lot. When I say a lot... I mean day and night. He worked
18. at some factory job in the day and then left the house
19. most nights to be a security guard. He would always
20. bring me home little surprises. Nothing expensive. Just
21. little things like fresh baked bagels still warm from the
22. baker. On Sundays, in the summer, he gave me money to
23. get ice cream from the corner candy store. I never had
24. to ask. He would say... here, go get yourself an ice cream
25. and flip me some money. He never got angry at me that
26. I can remember... well maybe once when I touched his
27. security gun. I didn't even take it out of its black leather
28. holster. It was too cold and too heavy. I just touched
29. it. When he saw that... he raised his voice loud like a

30. cannon. It scared the hell out of me. I tried not to cry
31. but my lip had a mind of its own and started to quiver,
32. then the tears started to roll. He pulled me over close to
33. him. And for a moment I thought he might hit me but
34. that wasn't it at all. He pulled me close and hugged me
35. I'm sorry he said. Then he reached in his shirt pocket
36. and pulled out a crumpled bill and said: Go get yourself
37. an ice cream. He never ever said anything to me about
38. going to college.

39. He was just happy to let me be what I was... a kid.

(Beat)

40. When I look back at it now, I think my father was always
41. with me in the present moment. Whatever or wherever
42. I was at that moment in time, that's where he was. He
43. was that way until the day he died... and that meant a lot
44. to me.

(Beat)

45. I mean why should a five year old kid have to think about
46. going to college? What the hell is that about? Can you
47. imagine... today is your birthday Johnny, now make a
48. wish and blow out **all of the** candles. And remember
49. you should work hard and not play too much. Because
50. too much play will rot your brain! Be number one in
51. your kindergarten class and eliminate all competitors
52. Get nothing less than an A on all of your report cards
53. because anything less (especially B or B+) would mean
54. you're a loser. Go to college but not just any college...
55. a top ten Ivy League college... Then a top law school...
56. With a scholarship!

(Beat)

57.   Now blow!

#16 PERFUME AND PEANUTS (MALE)

(Holding a brown paper bag)

1. You ever shake hands with someone and then have the
2. smell of their cologne or perfume on *your* hand? It's
3. always bothered me but for some reason it bothers me
4. more now than it used to. I'm not sure why? Maybe
5. I've become more sensitive to certain types of smell or
6. maybe perfumes and colognes just don't smell as good
7. as they used to? There is also the possibility that society
8. has become so hardened that we just drench ourselves
9. with perfume and cologne so that people will notice us?
10. Whatever the reason is, when I am in close contact with
11. these types of people soaked in let's call them offensive
12. odors, I have an allergic reaction. My eyes start to tear,
13. the roof of my mouth gets itchy and sometimes... my
14. throat starts to close. I am definitely allergic to most of
15. these scents like Aquolina or Aramis. As soon as I sense
16. the smell, it's already too late. My body starts a complex
17. rejection process which culminates in my feeling ill for
18. the rest of the day. You might think, just walk away from
19. the smell or if it's on your hand just wash it off. Not so easy,
20. they make this stuff so it sticks to you. As soon as you smell
21. it, thousands of tiny little perfume molecules are working
22. their way up your nostrils, into your lungs and processed
23. into your blood stream. My brain is sending a message to
24. my lungs... shut down! Emergency! Emergency! You're a
25. goner.

(Beat)

26. I'm getting a reaction just thinking about it. Thankfully
27. for most people, allergies from pollen, flowers and

28. smog... are merely a seasonal annoyance. But you know
29. I saw on TV... on one of those news shows that for many
30. of the estimated 11 million Americans who suffer from
31. allergies, that an allergic reaction can be life threatening.
32. So you could get stuck on an elevator next to one of
33. these stinkoids and risk your life. To avoid odor - induced
34. anaphylaxis – a sudden, severe, potentially fatal allergic
35. response – you have got to be constantly vigilant about
36. what kinds of smells you encounter.

37. In fact, avoidance of the problem by not putting yourself
38. in harms way is currently the only truly safe way to deal
39. with the problem. That means not sitting next to anyone
40. with Palmade in their hair at movie theaters, staying away
41. from cosmetic departments at the mall and especially
42. staying away from old people.

(Beat)

43. For some reason senior citizens really pour it on. Don't
44. really know why... but they do. Now, what if after taking
45. all these precautions, you get nailed by some stinkoid just
46. walking on the street. They bump into you and BAM!
47. You've got the smell all over you! It's on your hands, in
48. your eyes, on your clothing just working its way into your
49. blood stream and lungs. Always carry an emergency dose
50. of epinephrine. Drop some of that as soon as you come
51. into contact and you just might make it through. What
52. can I say? Life is like a rat maze full of dangers. It's not
53. an easy way to live but you do it. And... you got to look
54. at the bright side. You could be allergic to peanuts... now
55. if those peanut people eat just one nut their whole body
56. goes into a seizure and they die! Pretty harsh... not being
57. able to eat peanut butter and jelly sandwiches.

(Takes sandwich out of bag and takes a big bite.)

58.   I'd take a perfume allergy any day over that.

#17 THE REAL SANTA (MALE)

1. You probably think this is a joke, but I met the *real* Santa
2. Claus once when I was about six or seven. I was at Macy's
3. Department store in Long Island. I waited on line with
4. a bunch of other kids for about ten minutes ready to go
5. through the candy cane gates and up the steps for the
6. usual sit on the lap.

(Beat, sit)

7. My biggest problem at that time was whether or not I was
8. going to get a Diver Dan Frogman boat or a Tommy Gun
9. that I saw on television. At that age... what you ask Santa
10. for Christmas is a life decision. There was some kid in
11. front of me chewing Bazooka Bubble gum way too loud.
12. You could tell it was Bazooka Gum... by the way it smelled.
13. I wasn't a normal kid in the fact that I didn't chew gum
14. because I didn't like the way it sounded in your mouth.
15. I'm still that way today... don't like gum or gum snappers
16. for that matter. But that day, all that I could think of was
17. how much I wanted the Diver Dan, just like my friend
18. Giro Carbone had. Giro kept his wrapped up in the box
19. it came in. He would take it out and play Diver Dan in his
20. bath tub and wrap it up again in the box and hide it in
21. the back of his bedroom closet. He brought into school
22. one day for show and tell but he wouldn't let anybody
23. touch it... well except Mary Zito. She was one grade ahead
24. of us and he had the hots for her. So he let Mary take
25. the Diver Dan out of the box and hold it up to the light.
26. She said: Diver Dan... is just a diver... that's boring! What
27. an idiot! If Mary Zito had even an ounce of sense in her
28. brain she would know that Diver Dan was no ordinary
29. diver... he could swim on both the surface and under

30. water under his own propulsion. Jeeze... Mary, you little
31. twit, Diver Dan could dive to the depths of the ocean and
32. wrestle with giant octopuses on his adventures of looking
33. for buried treasure hidden below a sunken ship. So I just
34. had to have a Diver Dan...

(Beat)

35. The Tommy gun, was also pretty neat. It had a black
36. handle that you could pull back and get a real machine
37. gun sound. It was modeled after the machine gun they
38. used at the Saint Valentines Day massacre... I remember
39. seeing it on TV on the Untouchables. It was stylish type
40. of weapon. Black on black which meant it could match
41. almost anything you were wearing. This was a must have
42. toy to have when you were playing guns... you could kill
43. several of the enemy all at once... all with that wonderful
44. rat tat tat sound effect. What can I say? I had to have it.

(Beat)

45. I soon realized that I was almost next on line. I had been
46. to the Santa Claus line before. I knew the drill. My mom
47. told me... "these department store Santa's are Santa's
48. helpers... they help Santa out at Christmas time. Santa
49. only stops at certain department stores." And I thought to
50. myself... which stores? I mean, how does Santa pick which
51. stores he stops at. Does he go to Bloomingdales or Macys?
52. Anyway, every kid knows the drill with the Santa's helper.
53. He says "Ho Ho Ho" and then asks if you had been a good
54. boy. Then, all you had to do is reply "Yes... Santa!" And
55. then you would tell him what you want for Christmas just
56. loud enough so your parents could hear it ... and go buy
57. it for you. That was pretty much it.

(Beat)

58. Just as my turn came up. I decided to go for broke and ask
59. this Santa's Helper for both the Diver Dan and the Tommy
60. Gun. I figured what the heck, give it a shot. I sat on his lap,
61. ready to go. He said: "Ho Ho Ho" and then popped the
62. question. "Have you been a good boy?" I replied: "Sure
63. Santa! I'll take the Diver Dan and the Tommy Gun"... He
64. looked at me close and his eyes seemed to pierce right
65. through me like Superman's Xray vision. "Not so fast." He
66. said. "I happen to know you have not been a good boy.
67. You've been a bad boy sometimes, haven't you?" My first
68. thought this joker didn't even know my name... I thought
69. about telling him he was getting me mixed up with some
70. other kid. But this was New York... and no respectable
71. New York kid would go down without a fight. "Santa... how
72. do you know if I've been bad or good? You're just one
73. of Santa's helpers... am I right or what?" He smiled and
74. shook his head and said "nice try kid... but you're talking
75. to the Real Santa... Ho Ho Ho!" I knew then, that I was
76. busted. He was not a helper. He was the real deal... the real
77. santa. He seemed to know everything. When I asked if he
78. knew about the times I cursed in the school yard, or when
79. I put dog crap on Joseph Kolbrecher's new shirt and when
80. I hit Diane Mankowitz in the back of the head with a snow
81. ball causing her to lose her retainer. He shook his head
82. in acknowledgment. He knew it all. I said: "What's this all
83. mean? Am I going to get a lump of coal?" He laughed not
84. a Ho Ho Ho but the kind of laugh you get when you know
85. you're in trouble and at someone elses mercy.

86. I pleaded with him: "What going to happen to me?" He
87. smiled: "Have a lollipop!" And before I could pick a red
88. one, he handed me a yellow lemon lollipop. I hated yellow

89. lemon lollipops but took it anyway. I said: "Jeeze Santa,
90. I'm sorry..., do you ever give a kid a break?" He didn't say
91 a word. He just patted me on the head as I slid off his lap.
92. I headed down the ramp toward the exit thinking maybe
93. I could come back in a day or so and try to smooth things
94. out. Just as I got to the candy cane gates which lead back
95. into the toy department, he called out to me. "Hey kid...
96. Say hello to Diver Dan!" I thought to myself... this guy
97. still doesn't know my real name... there might be some
98. daylight here? I smiled as I turned to him and said: "Sure
99. thing... Santa." I took off as fast as I could because I was
100. afraid he might change his mind. I knew then that I had
101. met the real Santa.

#18 B. I. Y. A. (FEMALE)

(**Enter holding a paper grocery bag**)

1. Did you ever do something that was horribly stupid that
2. you can't believe it? It has happened to almost all of us at
3. one time or another. There's no specific condition that we
4. suffer. We're just a normal person functioning as best as
5. can be expected when suddenly one of these really stupid
6. events envelops us and we stand there saying to ourselves:
7. Shit, I can't believe I just did that!

(**Beat**)

8. This is what I will call B. Y. I. A. for BRAINS IN YOUR
9. ASS. In certain circles, it is also referred to as S. F. B. or
10. SHIT FOR BRAINS. Essentially, describes those singular
11. moments when all the reason and intelligence you have
12. in your brain, is suddenly transferred literally to your ass.
13. Ergo, the name B. Y. I. A.

(**Beat**)

14. How and why does it occur? Don't know. It just does. It
15. can be the result of diet but there is no research that
16. indicates that certain diets of proteins or carbohydrates
17. facilitate the experience. Mind-altering substances are
18. often blamed for B. I. Y. A. But the truth of it is, if you
19. have had a few drinks and say something ridiculous
20. that is a totally different experience. In this case, your
21. senses have been dulled by a particular substance such
22. as alcohol. Your brain is otherwise functioning normally
23. until you drug the crap out it and inhibit its ability to
24. reason. B. I. Y. A. is a totally different occurrence. No

25.   mind altering substances of any kind are involved. This
26.   is a pure transference of function from brain to ass. Oh,
27.   here's another example, you may be walking down the
28.   street and an African American man walks up to you and
29.   asks for directions to the subway and you say Your people
30.   have suffered one hundred and fifty years of oppression
31.   under the whip of their white masters. Plymouth Rock
32.   definitely landed on you. It's two blocks down on the
33.   right-hand side... right by the pretzel vendor.

(Beat)

34.   Another example: You're at a cocktail type party where
35.   alcohol is involved but you are not partaking in the apple
36.   martini stingers being served. You're talking about the
37.   price of gasoline when you suddenly blurt out I just can't
38.   figure it out... when they build a gas station... how do they
39.   know where to drill... I mean how do they know there's
40.   going to be oil underneath... do they drill first or build
41.   the gas station first? You say this quite loudly but no one
42.   answers because they are all inebriated on the Apple
43.   Martini's. But the fact still remains that your mindless
44.   statement is the result of B. I. Y. A.

(Beat)

45.   Now that you know what it is, how do you prevent it.
46.   Answer. You can't! There is no way clinically to prevent
47.   this from happening and no known cure. So what is
48.   to be done? When B. I. Y. A. occurs don't fight it... just
49.   let it happen and as the Ancient Greek Sophists would
50.   say... go with the flow. When the B. I. Y. A. phenomenon
51.   overtakes you, go with it! Take the journey and take it with
52.   conviction. Some of you may say... isn't this just Bull Shit.

53. And some might say Yes... it is... But think of politicians...
54. they have chronic attacks of B. I. Y. A. almost daily... and
55. the only difference between you and them is they get paid
56. to do it. And they do it with conviction. So, you do the
57. same.... and people just might listen... and who knows?
58. You might just get elected too!

(Put the bag over your head and EXIT)

#19 THE WAY HE PUT JELLY ON BREAD (FEMALE)

1. I was married, the first time, when I was eighteen. That
2. was a *long* time ago... seems so far away to me. As if it really
3. wasn't me that did it. It wasn't one of those weddings with
4. the bride all in white in church with a choir. Nothing like
5. that at all. It was more of a spur of the moment type of
6. event. There was this guy Bobbie, who was about a year
7. older than me and the lead singer of this house band of
8. this club I used to go to. He wasn't much of what I would
9. call a looker kind of average height with long dark hair.
10. He always wore a paisley shirt tucked in with a black belt
11. and black boots. The club was called the Daisy with lots
12. day glow yellow flowers painted on the outside and even
13. more on the walls and ceiling and a large bar and a stage
14. where the band played. The Daisy was one of those places
15. that you could get into if you were under age. They never
16. just came out and said it... but everybody knew that the
17. owner Sal never asked for ID. I could get in there and
18. drink even though I wasn't twenty-one. Pretty good deal...
19. when you're only eighteen.

(Beat)

20. Every Friday night I would go there, hang out at the bar
21. nursing a rum and coke. And every Friday night, the house
22. band would play hit songs and Bobbie would sing most of
23. the leads or just hang up there and play a tambourine and
24. sing backup harmony. On this particular Friday night,
25. the band did a new song by the band Chicago... he sang
26. Color My World I'm sure you know the song... it was a
27. great slow dance or bum and grind number depending on
28. who you were dancing with. The first part of the song was

29.   instrumental and then when it was repeated it a second
30.   time, Bobbie sang the lead vocal... but he didn't just sing
31.   it... he sang it just to me.

(Sings)

32.   *As time goes on I realize just what you mean to me ...*
33.   *And now... now that you're near...*

34.   So on and so forth. It felt so cool when he did that...
35.   everybody in the club knew it too. I felt so special my body
36.   got numb and tingly all over. Now that I'm older, I think
37.   it was probably because I had a few too many rum and
38.   cokes... but back then, it was all Bobbie. At that moment
39.   in time, when he sang the words Color my world with love
40.   ... just to me, I wanted to scream out loud... Okay! I'll
41.   color your world with love! At that very moment... I loved
42.   him as much as any woman could love a man.

(Beat)

43.   After Color My World, the band took a half hour break.
44.   We'll be right back... and Bobbie jumped down off of the
45.   stage, and asked me to take a walk with him out in the
46.   parking lot. I did... we walked for a while and finally sat
47.   back on the hood of his 67 Camaro. We both looked up at
48.   the night sky and talked about lots of things two people talk
49.   about when they look up at the stars... love, relationships,
50.   high school and going to war. Bobbie graduated one
51.   year before I did and really wasn't interested in going
52.   to college. He just wanted to sing in the band and have
53.   a good time. That by itself would not have been a big
54.   deal except that there was a war going on in Vietnam and
55.   Bobbie got tagged for the draft. I heard he was scheduled

56. to report for basic training but I didn't know when. He
57. said: I've got to report for basic training... I'm going to
58. Nam. When I asked when. He said tomorrow morning. I
59. stopped in my tracks and figured I know what's happening
60. here. This guy is going into the army tomorrow morning
61. and wants to have one last fling tonight! I pulled away.
62. But just as I did, he spoke.

(Beat)

63. That's when he told me he loved me. It came out of
64. nowhere... "I love you." And hit me like a lightening bolt.
65. And before I could recover... he hit me with... "and I want
66. to marry you... now... I mean tonight" I don't remember
67. what I said... I do remember that I looked up at the night
68. sky and saw a shooting star... That's all I remember. Not
69. much more.

(Beat)

70. It wasn't much of a ceremony. There was this Greek
71. family that owned a grocery store. The lived in the back
72. and their grandfather who also lived there, was a justice
73. of the peace. The Greek family cried when we said I do.
74. We had to hug and kiss every one of them even though
75. we didn't know their names. There must have been ten
76. of them counting cousins and grand parents. Then they
77. asked us to take some groceries and Bobbie took a jar
78. of peanut butter, one jar of grape jelly, a loaf of white
79. bread and a carton of milk. He tried to pay for it all but
80. they refused to take any money. Everyone started to cry
81. one more time and we hugged and kissed them all again.
82. When we finally left, the guys in the band by the doorway
83. and sang Color My World and threw Uncle Ben's rice on

84. us as we got into Bobbie's Camaro. We planned to drive
85. to Atlantic City by the shore but never made it. There just
86. wasn't enough time. We pulled off the highway into the
87. parking lot of a tattered road side motel which was next
88. to a drive in movie. I don't know how anyone could get
89. any sleep in that motel because the movie screen was so
90. large and so close... you hear the sound from the speakers
91 in the parking lot. It was like being *in* the drive in without
92. being in the drive in.

(Beat)

93. We started to get a room but never made it. We started
94. watching the movie at first from the parking lot and
95. then later we climbed up on the hood of the Camaro so
96. we could see the whole screen. I can't remember what
97. movie it was... maybe a war movie with Gregory Peck
98. but I just don't know. After a while, we got hungry and
99. Bobbie took out the jar of peanut butter and jelly and
100. made sandwiches. I couldn't help but notice how serious
101. he got when he put the jelly on the bread. He held the
102. bread flat in his hand and spread the jelly evenly across
103. the bread right up to the crust until the piece of bread
104. was covered right up to the edge. But the funny part was,
105. he never once let the jelly touch the crust. When I told
106. him that he said That's the kind of guy I am I'm going to
107. live my life to the fullest... spread the jelly all you want but
108. never ever let it touch the crust... never.

(Beat)

109. The next morning, Bobbie dropped me off at home on
110. his way to basic. The sun barely lit the morning sky and
111. my parents were still asleep when I held Bobbie close. It

112. was one of those awkward moments when you really don't
113. know what to say. I was about to say goodbye when he cut
114. me off and kissed me instead and then whispered Wait for
115. me. My eyes followed his Camaro go down the street until
116. it disappeared around the corner. I never saw Bobbie
117. again. He was killed in action.

(Beat)

118. For several years, I saw his face in my mind whispering
119. Wait for me... and I thought that by some miracle that it
120. was all a mistake and that he would show up at my door
121. step in his paisley shirt. Things like that happen all the
122. time in war.

123. But the passage of time is so final... it moves forward...
124. never back... and I moved on with my life... two marriages...
125. children and now grand children... And Bobbie?

126. Do you want to know the truth? I can't remember what he
127. looked like. His face... his eyes... his touch... I just can't. Is
128. that a terrible thing? I'm sorry Bobbie. Very sorry.

(Beat)

129. But, if I reach deep down in my soul to a place to the
130. center of who I am... who I became... I do remember one
131. thing about Bobbie... just like it was yesterday.

132. Spread the jelly all you want but never ever let it touch the
133. crust... That's the way *he* put jelly on bread.

(Smile then exit.)

#20 BREAKING UP (MALE)

1. I have tried to break up with this girl Susan for at least a
2. month now. But every time I have tried to do it, it doesn't
3. work out. Like last night, I was really an ass hole, talked
4. out loud a lot during the movie about the credits... who
5. the best boy was and who directed... who the hell cares?
6. And what does a best boy do anyway? I figured it would
7. embarrass her... not a chance. Then after the movie, we're
8. walking out and she said how much she loved it... and that
9. it was so *ROMANTIC*. I snapped back and said it was a
10. panzi assed sappy left wing chick flick... just a bunch of
11. talking heads I didn't care about. And what's with the sub
12. titles? How can people read and watch a movie at the same
13. time? I'm a visual person... give me Kung Fucking Foo
14. with guns blazing and lots of gratuitous sex and violence.
15. Now that's what makes me happy. I knew saying all that
16. would piss her off... I went on to say how I hated anything
17. remotely romantic and how anyone who was romantic in
18. the modern world was a total loser... and that they would
19. **live** a loser ... and **die** a loser. (Beat) That should of got
20. her... right there... But, no response! So I said... Maybe
21. you're so brain dead... you didn't get it the first time, so
22. I here it is again... IT WAS A PIECE OF CRAP! I said it
23. as loud as I could... then walked away from her. I figured
24. right there was where she'd flip me the bird... and I could
25. say FINE HAVE IT YOUR WAY! But she just stood there...
26. frozen stiff... with her eyes wide open... didn't say a word.
27. Ya'know like a squirrel does in the forest when they don't
28. want you to see them... you ever see that? (stands like
29. a frozen squirrel) I saw a documentary about that on
30. Animal Planet. The little bush tailed fuckers think they're
31. invisible... and she was standing there doing the same
32. thing! Frozen stiff... and it was kind of ticking me off to

33. the point where I was actually starting to feel glad I was
34. finally breaking up with this comatose moron!   So I said:
35. Enough of this crap... I'm outta here!

(Beat)

36. That's the break away line. I made a hard left rudder
37. and did a bee line to my car, got in and slammed the
38. door (real hard) like I was gonna explode. I actually was
39. okay but I thought the door slam would add dramatic
40. effect. I started the engine and figured she follow me and
41. open the passenger door and get in. But, she didn't. She
42. was still out there in front of the theater... frozen like a
43. fucking squirrel... It really started to piss me off. (Beat)
44. Then, I thought to myself... this was actually a good thing.
45. This was the straw that broke the camel's back... this was
46. it! I did it... Did I do it? Yeah... I did! I BROKE UP WITH
47. HER... I'm out! I am finally fucking out of six months of
48. bondage and oppression. I'm finally out! Free! I revved
49. my engine and gunned it... My tires left a little rubber
50. as I peeled away. Also, for dramatic effect. I was G O
51. N E... as I pulled away I saw her in my rearview mirror
52. still doing the squirrel thing. As I drove, her image got
53. smaller and smaller until it vanished. I couldn't believe it
54. was that easy! I'm done. A free man. I popped on the CD
55. player for some freedom music! (Beat) It played the song
56. I heard the day I first time I met her... she was standing
57. behind me at the Eight Items Only Line and she said
58. Excuse me... I think you have nine items... and should
59. get the hell out of this line. At the time, I thought that
60. was the cutest thing.

(Beat)

61. I was almost a block away and it hit me like a ton of bricks
62. BAM. I started to feel bad about what I did... ya'know
63. the door slam and the whole squirrel thing... and then
64. I thought about the little things... like the way she made
65. a mustache over her lip when she drank a cappuccino...
66. and the way she smelled like Binaca right after she washed
67. her hair. I love that smell.

(Beat)

68. The further I drove away from her the worse I felt. I
69. started breathing heavy, and got a lump in my throat like
70. I was going to hurl. (Beat) I slammed on the brakes and
71. spun my car around. When I turned the corner, she was
72. running along the street. I pulled up next to her and
73. shouted out the window "Hop in!"

(Beat)

74. She got in the car and said: "Let's get an ice cream, I'm
75. starving." I shrugged my shoulders: "Sure thing"...As we
76. drove off, I felt relieved and sad all at the same time. There
77. I was back in the saddle... like I never left. Then I thought
78. of a line that Al Pacino said in Godfather III which went
79. something like "Every time I try to get out... I get pulled
80. back in." (Beat) What can I say... I just couldn't break up
81. with her. Not this time anyway... maybe tomorrow.

(Exit)

#21 BREAKING UP (FEMALE)

1. I have tried to break up with this guy Bradley for at least
2. a month now. But so far, no such luck. I did the cold and
3. condescending bitch routine but I think he likes it? For
4. instance, last night we went to the movies. I insisted on
5. going to a movie I knew he would HATE … We saw this
6. panzi assed sappy left wing chick flick... just a bunch of
7. talking heads I didn't care about. And what's with the
8. sub titles? How can people read and watch a movie at
9. the same time? I'm a visual person... give me Brad Pitt or
10. Johnny Depp a Greek toga or a Kung Foo movie and I'm
11. happy. But I did it just to piss him off and to put salt in the
12. wound, I went on and on how wonderfully romantic it was.
13. He said he hated all things romantic... no surprise there.
14. Bradley was as romantic as a dead gold fish floating on
15. top of the bowl. He tried to kiss me once, but I was able to
16. fend him off by spraying my hair with Binaca... really did
17. the trick. He had an allergic reaction and fell asleep. After
18. the movie, I thought I go for the final kill. I decided to rig
19. for silent running and no matter what he said to me not
20. say a word back. I didn't act mad or anything... I just didn't
21. respond. No matter what he said... I just stood there. I
22. figured that would make him mad and it did... and he
23. really started to go off on me. I could hardly stay silent...
24. I really wanted to tell him that he was a blood sucking
25. mama's boy loser and would never amount to anything. I
26. was just about to say **that** when he just walked off to his car,
27. got in, slammed the door and peeled off. (Beat) I said to
28. myself... this ass hole just stranded me here without a ride
29. home... But, if you look at the big picture... this is a good
30. thing. I didn't make a move! Because I figured any such
31. movement might make him change his mind and come
32. back. So I stood there... frozen... with my eyes frozen wide

33. open, you know like a squirrel does when they don't want
34. you to see them. Like this... (Take a frozen squirrel pose)
35. I saw a documentary about that on the Animal Planet.
36. Once he was out of sight, I got out my cell phone and
37. called some of my friends. I was going to meet them and
38. get an ice cream, I was starving. I started to walk away
39. when I heard the screeching sound of his Bradley's tires...
40. and said to myself SHIT HE's BACK... and this is hell. I
41. thought to myself, I can run or throw myself in front of
42. the car and end it quick. I started to run away. But it was
43. too late... there he was,... riding right next to me with his
44. window open, he shouted: Hop in! (Beat) What could I
45. do? I was trapped like a rat running in a maze. I got in...
46. He smiled at me and I was happy and sad all at once...
47. happy because I wasn't running and sad... because I had
48. failed. Then I thought of a line that Al Pacino said in
49. Godfather III... an inferior film to the first two. The line
50. went something like this: Every time I try to get away from
51. this ass hole... he catches me. Maybe that wasn't the right
52. line... but it fit at that moment. Then, I said: "Let's get an
53. ice cream, I'm starving." And he said: "Sure thing"... As
54. we drove off I thought to myself, didn't make it tonight...
55. I just couldn't break up with him. Maybe tomorrow.

#22 FIRST IMPRESSION #1 (FEMALE)

1. My first impression of him was … what a loser! The way
2. his hair stood up and the kind of goofy look he had on his
3. face when he said: Hey what's **your** name? His lips were
4. moving but I didn't hear a word he said. I kept thinking
5. to myself How am I going to get to the door without him
6. thinking I was a stuck up bitch? It's important to me what
7. people think of me. I don't want them to think bad things
8. about me. I'm a good person. So I hung out with him for
9. a while and you know what? He wasn't such a loser after
10. all. He was just kind of weird. But in a cute sort of way …
11. and **that** I like.

#23 FIRST IMPRESSION #2 (FEMALE)

1. When I first meet somebody, I kind of gravitate to one
2. part of their body. I don't want you to think I'm some
3. sort of pervert, but that's what happens. I have absolutely
4. no control over it. It just happens as naturally as the sun
5. rising in the morning.

(Beat)

6. I met this guy the other day when I was on line at the
7. bank. He was behind me and we started talking about
8. something like I'd rather be at the beach... instead of
9. waiting on this line and how I usually use the ready teller
10. machine because I hate waiting on line but couldn't today
11. because the check I was trying to cash wasn't actually
12. made out in *my* name and that the name on the check
13. was a fictitious one that I only use at work because I don't
14. want any of the freaks there to know what my real name
15. was... because they were all a bunch of moron stalkers
16. and would probably find out where I lived and try to
17. break into my house and steal my underwear... and then
18. it hit me STOP!

(Beat)

19. I'm giving this guy WAY TOO MUCH information.
20. But I did so because I was in a relaxed state while I was
21. talking to him and that was because I was looking at his
22. mouth. He had a yellowed chip on one of his front teeth
23. (maybe a cavity) and the teeth as a whole were a bit yellow
24. (probably from smoking or poor oral hygiene or being
25. English) but his teeth and mouth were my comfort zone
26. with this particular person. No matter what he was doing

27.   or wearing that's the place my eyes would go. I have no
28.   idea why, but focusing on his mouth made me feel more
29.   comfortable than let's say looking into his eyes. His eyes,
30.   for whatever reason, just didn't do it for me. I don't even
31.   recall whether they were brown or blue.

(Beat)

32.   There were only two people ahead of me in line so I didn't
33.   have time to experiment with body parts. I went right for
34.   the part of his body that made me feel comfortable. His
35.   mouth. My first impression of him was… nice mouth Now
36.   that doesn't sound like much… but when you're on line
37.   at the bank and you only have a minute or two… that's a
38.   lot.

(Beat)

39.   I could tell he was just about to ask me my name when a
40.   buzzer sounded indicating it was my turn. My eyes jerked
41.   away from him to the television screen next to the bank
42.   tellers to see an arrow with the number eight under it.
43.   At that moment, all bets were off and our conversation
44.   changed to one of meaning to one of what I call platitudes
45.   of completion… Well… have a great day… Have a great
46.   weekend… Well… see you around and don't spend all your
47.   money in one place. What the hell do those statements
48.   really mean?

(Beat)

49.   This is what they mean… Well pal, my turn is up… and
50.   that's more important than you. My turn is after all why
51.   I'm here. This puny check I have to cash that is made out

52. to a fictitious person other than myself is more important
53. than *you*. So have a nice life pal. Maybe I'll see you on line
54. again? That would be special. Something like that. But
55. you know you'll... NEVER see him on line again in just
56. this way. Because the mathematical possibility of running
57. into this guy on the line at the bank in exactly the same
58. order is almost an impossibility! So, I know in my heart
59. that this is it! OVER! DONE! And... I'm really okay with
60. it because at this moment, my mind is already gone... even
61. though my body is still lingers. My brain is already trying
62. to come up with a plausible story to say to the bank teller
63. about why the check I want to cash is made out to a name
64. other than my own. THAT is the most important thing on
65. my mind at that moment in time.

66. Because without that check cashed, I am truly screwed.
67. I need the money for gas for my car so I can get to work
68. and earn a minimum wage and pay taxes and get deeper
69. into debt. NOW THAT's WHAT's IMPORTANT!

(Beat)

70. It's the American Way! And I'm not going to let anyone
71. or anything get in the way of that. Even if this guy seemed
72. nice and had a nice mouth. At least, that was my first
73. impression. But ya' never know.

#24 I WANT TO BE LIKE AN INDIAN (MALE)

(Holding Feather while dancing silently in a circle)

1. I want to be like an Indian... you know like one of those
2. Indians you see in the movies and on TV. The Noble
3. Savage who is *at one* with nature and the universe, who
4. never tells a lie, only kills when put in a life threatening
5. situation and only hunts animals for the purpose of eating
6. them for survival. No weekend hunters here! Indians only
7. hunted for food... and that's the way it should be. The
8. Indian had a reverence for the universe in which he lived.
9. You won't see any of those TV or Movie Indians polluting
10. the environment. They respect nature for what it is
11. beautiful, harsh and ever changing. That's what makes
12. Indians so cool...

(Beat)

13. I want to be like an Indian... with a name like... Crazy Dude
14. Wild Horse or Horny Like a Dog or Free Like the Eagle.
15. I love the thought of having a name that's a metaphor
16. instead of just plain old Joe... or Kyle... or even worse...
17. Chad. No one syllable name for me... oh no.

(Beat, make Indian gesture – holding hand up)

18. How! I am Chief Dick Like a Bat and these are my
19. people... Indians pick these free wheeling images because
20. they don't want to be encumbered by the chains of society.
21. Indians, at least on TV, don't have to sit in traffic on the
22. freeway... don't to pay taxes... and most importantly don't
23. worry about leaving the toilet seat up. Why? They're

24. Indians! They live under the stars like those wild horses
25. that you read about in National Geographic magazine...
26. running around the hills of Montana. The hills are their
27. home. They live with only the open sky over their heads
28. and the wind on their backs. They're free! And they wear
29. very cool suede clothes too!
30. That's me... an Indian
31. unchained
32. unfettered
33. unshackled
34. untied ... and the best part of it is... if somebody pisses you
35. off... you can just scalp em with your tomahawk!

(Beat)

36. That's why I want to be like an Indian... at least an Indian
37. like you see on TV or the Movies.

(War whoops)

38. WHOOO HAAA! HAAA! HAAA!

(EXIT)

#25 THE BACKSIDE OF YOUR HEAD (MALE)

(Looking at the back side of head by holding two small mirrors)

1.   You ever look at the back of your head? I mean I really
2.   never spent much time thinking about the *back side of my*
3.   *head*... I had all to do with trying to get the *front of my head*
4.   together. I would look in the mirror before I went out the
5.   door and check myself out... teeth, hair, nose ears, eyes
6.   ... then I'd say okay... and then be gone. I thought I was
7.   okay *but that was until* I saw myself in one of those mirrors
8.   where you're able to see the back of your head at the same
9.   time as the front. Let me tell you, it was amazing. My
10. head from the back looked as big as a basketball, my hair
11. was flat, and my ears looked like a taxi cab going down
12. the street with its doors open. I was in a state of shock
13. thinking that *all this time* I was working on the front of me
14. when I should've been working on the back... that's the
15. last thing people see when they look at you. And the last
16. thing they see is what they remember the most.

(Beat)

17. Think about **that**, next time you look in the mirror.

#26 DOG's FEET SMELL LIKE POPCORN (FEMALE)

1.   Did you ever notice that if you smell the underside of dry
2.   dog feet... they smell just like popcorn? Not the microwave
3.   kind with the burn't smell... but the kind of popcorn you
4.   get at the movies. You know... that fresh roasted smell...
5.   smothered with butter. Nice and toasty...

(Beat – take a sniff)

6.   I love that smell... and that's probably why I like dog's so
7.   much... because their feet smell like popcorn. I've never
8.   really been able to figure out. They just do... it's just one
9.   of those scientific facts... dogs' feet smell like popcorn. I
10.   mean what's that all about anyway?

(Beat)

11.   Why don't my feet smell like popcorn after I've been
12.   walking around all day? It's a mystery... and breath...
13.   did you ever smell a dog's breath... is it heaven or what?
14.   Especially puppy breath... no matter what they eat... and
15.   believe me they eat lots of things they probably shouldn't...
16.   their breath always smells... well... like puppy's breath. I
17.   think it would be great if people smelled like different
18.   foods. Imagine coming home after working all day and
19.   smelling like pumpkin pie or vanilla ice cream? Wouldn't
20.   that be nice? Or maybe not... nobody would ever take a
21.   shower. I guess that's not such a good idea after all.

#27 THE TROUBLE WITH TWO (FEMALE)

1. The trouble with two
2. is it falls between one and three
3. One is just **one**
4. it doesn't have to do anything but
5. just be **one**
6. **one** is what everyone wants to be
7. **number one**
8. And three
9. is the latest model you have just got to have
10. the shiny red convertible... "Did you see the new 3?
11. Is it hot or what?
12. the improved
13. the strongest
14. the lat of the trinity
15. timeless and unending
16. synergistic and harmonious
17. that's why it's **three.**
18. But two
19. is just in the middle
20. indifferent
21. passed by
22. victimized by progress
23. the unreachable center
24. the balance never achieved
25. sitting on the line between
26. ying and yang
27. good and bad
28. black and white
29. brown and yellow
30. let's face it two is
31. nowhere
32. no one remembers number two.

33. Two is there to make us feel bad
34. about ourselves
35. It draws the lines between
36. our differences – he's "one" and well... you're just "two"
37. You should have worked a little harder, then you wouldn't
38. be number "two."
39. Two reminds us
40. that we're not where or who we're supposed to be
41. we're behind number one
42. one is the best
43. we're just two
44. part of the larger group
45. the mediocrats
46. the disenfranchised
47. the taken for granted
48. the would've could've crowd
49. spending our life waiting on line
50. to do what we have to do
51. rather than what we dream
52. That's the trouble with two

(Beat, Exit – then Return)

53. No, that's not right.
54. The truth is that
55. Two
56. is the glue that binds the
57. universe together
58. connecting the void
59. to the reality
60. That's number two!
61. Two
62. round
63. and

64. curved over
65. flat bottomed
66. and
67. solidly in the middle of it all.
68. Keeping the balance
69. in a world ready to tip over
70. at a moments notice.
71. Two…

(EXIT)

#28 WHITE SILHOUETTE (MALE)

(A lonely violin echoes in the distance)

1. Dance with me
2. up close
3. with our eyes touching
4. kindly
5. upon our
6. souls
7. true intent

8. softly in the night

9. Dance with me
10. up close
11. underneath the stars and
12. moon
13. and blackened
14. night sky

15. your hand in mine

16. Dance with me
17. up close
18. your gown spinning lace
19. soft
20. the sweet
21. night air

22. like an angel's wings

23. Dance with me
24. up close
25. my love my only
26. one
27. in my
28. dream like
29. a fleeting white silhouette

#29 YOU CAN PICK YOUR FRIENDS...

(Holding a potted plant)

1. Have you ever heard the saying... You can pick your
2. friends but you can't pick your relatives? This on its
3. face values tells us that our relatives... mothers, fathers,
4. brothers, sisters, aunts, uncles and cousins are irrevocably
5. bound to us by blood ties (in other words you're stuck)
6. and that our relationships with the people who inhabit
7. the rest of the world are totally of our own choosing. But
8. let's talk reality here... do you actually think you can pick
9. your friends? (BEAT) Have you *ever* had the experience
10. of picking a friend? You can get on the phone and call
11. Bill Gates Hey Bill... what's up? And he says... Dude...
12. how's it going... pool party at my house... tomorrow night!
13. Or better yet, call Tom Cruise say Since I've selected you
14. to be my friend, I would like you to put me in your next
15. movie. After all, what are friends for? (Beat) Ever done
16. that? Don't think so... As if to say we have any choice at
17. all in who we associate with? The truth is neither Bill
18. Gates or Tom Cruise would give you the right time of day.
19. Reason? As they would say: Who the hell are you? Do I
20. know you? You could try to say: No, I've never met you
21. until this moment but I've chosen you to be my friend. See
22. how far that gets you. (Beat) Friendship is mutual... and
23. requires the agreement of both parties... like a contract.
24. Any lawyers out there? I hope not... then we might be
25. here all night. Where was I?

(Beat)

26. Right... you can try to pick your friends but it doesn't
27. always mean that they will always pick you back. And

28. don't you hate when that happens? You extend yourself
29. in friendship... you lay your heart down on the line... and
30. they say... No thanks... I couldn't possibly be associated
31. with you. Be *your* friend? I don't think so... maybe with the
32. garbage can or the utility pole... but not with you. So we
33. try to hedge our bets a little... we gravitate to the familiar.
34. We pick people that are just like us.

(Beat)

35. We don't even know that we do it. The truth of it is... we
36. for the most part, have a tendency to mirror patterns
37. that are set in our psyche from birth. Don't ask me how I
38. know this... I think I read it somewhere in a magazine...
39. maybe Cosmopolitan or Popular Mechanics while I was
40. waiting to get my teeth cleaned at the dentist. Anyway,
41. as I remember it. We have certain associations that we
42. subconsciously seek out whether we know it or not ... In
43. short, we like ourselves, so we seek out people who are
44. just like us. Or ... Yes, there is an or to this... sometimes
45. we seek out people that are not necessarily like us but
46. rather people who serve a specific need that we must have
47. fulfilled because we love ourselves so much. Let me give
48. you a few examples... to support this.

(Beat)

49. Let's say... you not the type of person who is a leader or
50. driven to any specific goal... a couch potato, sloth type
51. individual who eats constantly and sleeps most of the time
52. while watching day time television. You know the type... A
53. LOSER. Losers want to befriend winners so they can *live*
54. vicariously through their achievements. In this sense, the
55. opposites attract concept comes into play. This is rooted

56. in the person's innate desire to be something other that
57. what they really are. So they seek out people that are their
58. opposites! It's the way of the universe. Leaders look for
59. followers, pretty girls' always have best friends that are
60. dogs. This is probably rooted in some primitive instinct
61. to survive that goes back to the cave man ... I didn't read
62. that... I just kind of made it up right now...

(Beat)

63. Also, let's not forget... Environmental friendships. You
64. don't get to pick these ... they are foisted upon you by
65. a particular environment. Places like the office, school,
66. or the gym also produce character types friends that are
67. labeled within those environments... such as the office
68. kiss ass or the office slut, the class clown, the uptight bitch
69. in payroll etc... we all know the labels and operate within
70. them.

(Beat)

71. Now, to the relatives part of the equation. Somehow all
72. the rules of picking go out the window... because you're
73. stuck with these people since birth... or so you believe.

(Beat)

74. I mean we all have the uncle that's a transvestite and is
75. getting a sex change operation in Sweden. Am I right?
76. Okay? You *must* at least have a cousin that works at Hooters
77. to help pay for her illegitimate toddler... and... of course
78. every family has at least one jail bird. That's a relative
79. that's been incarcerated for a period of time in a state or
80. federal institution.

81. We all have them... they're out there and we know it... we
82. just don't want anyone else to know it.

(Puts plant down.)

83. I wish relatives were as simple as a family tree... you could
84. just plant them really deep so the roots are tied to the
85. ground... give them plenty of water and sun light...

(Looks at it with pride)

86. Then... leave em.

(Exits)

#30 ISABELLA ALESSO –
January 17, 1937 (FEMALE)

(New York 30'S Period Dialect - holding book and pencil)

1. Diary... seventeen, January... nineteen thirty seven.
2. It must be almost midnight... and can't sleep... so I snuck
3. out of my bed and I came up on the roof and write in this
4. book. Ya... know... it's not a book ya read... the pages are
5. blank on the inside. It's my diaaree. Someday when I'm
6. older, I can read it and remember. I like it here on the
7. roof.. Very quiet except the pigeons and below you can
8. see the delivery trucks driving down the block. And above
9. you can see the sky and the whole city! If I lean just the
10. right way, I can get a clear shot of the new Empire State
11. Building! (Beat) I see all those lights up there glowing
12. against the sky at night like jewels. I specially want to see
13. the hole in the street where King Kong fell. Now that
14. was one monkey with moxie! I think he's swell and they
15. should've left him alone in the jungle. Instead they had to
16. shoot him down like a dog... it ain't right. (Beat) I want
17. to get up to the Empire State one day and see the hole in
18. the street Kong made when he fell. Don't want to sit here
19. on my culone while the whole world passes me by. I want
20. to be part of it all. But that's a long way from Mulberry
21. Street... but I'll get there! But for now, I'm happy to see it
22. from up here!

23. My apartment is just one floor below here because the
24. higher you go, the cheaper the rent! Have to climb all
25. the stairs... and let me tell you the tenth floor may not
26. sound so high to you... but there's are two flights of stairs
27. for each floor. Lots of climbing... but it's not so bad...
28. makes my gams strong and... you get to go on the roof

29. for some peace and quiet. Being the only girl with three
30. brothers means I got to sleep on a pull out bed in the
31. kitchen, which means last to go to sleep and first ta get
32. up. My brothers sleep in the bedroom all in one bed. At
33. least I get to sleep by myself.

(Beat)

34. My name is Isabella Alesso... my teacher Mrs. Simmons
35. calls me Isabel... but most of the kids at school call me
36. Izzy. I was named after my mother's older sister. She was
37. killed by a runaway horse and wagon in her village back
38. in Italy. I never met her but I know she was a real "Sheba"
39. her village and was supposed to marry this real big cheese
40. back there... and then suddenly wound up dead. It all
41. happened before I was born... but it was a pretty big deal.
42. My mother wanted to show her love for her only sister
43. by naming me after her! But I tell everybody that I was
44. named after the queen of Spain! Ya'know, Isabella.? The
45. one that was stuck on Christopher Columbus and sent
46. him off to discover America.

(Beat)

47. My father wanted to call me Juliette... ya'know like Romeo
48. and Juliet the play. But my father says... my mother's got a
49. head like a rock! So my mother won the fight.

(Beat)

50. I can't stay up this roof much longer. If my mother finds
51. out I came up here in the middle of the night, I'll get it
52. good. Besides, I've got to get up extra early tomorrow
53. because I have to get to school early. It's Parent's day

54. tomorrow and my father said her was going to come to
55. meet my teacher. I want to get to school real early and
56. make sure my desk is neat! It's not easy for him to come
57. to school because of his job. Has to take a train and a
58. ferry all the way to the New Jersey side of the River to
59. get to work in a factory that makes boxes that people put
60. jewelry in. They are all velvet outside and have a kind of
61. shiny material on the inside like a tiny coffin. His boss at
62. the factory, is giving him part of the day off, to come to
63. my school.

64. I got to make sure I'm ready when he gets there. My father
65. can speak English but not as good as he speaks Italian. I
66. want to be there when he talks to Mrs. Simmons so I can
67. help with the words she doesn't understand. I gotta go
68. back and go to sleep now. At least I'll try.
69. Izzy Alesso... January 17, 1937

#31 DETECTIVE GREEN – JULY 29, 2006 (MALE)

(New York Dialect)

1. My name is Detective Jerome Green, out of the 15th
2. Precinct, City of New York. My friends call me Jer but
3. since I don't really know you yet, just call me Detective
4. Green. If you haven't figured it out yet... yeah, I'm a
5. New Yorker. Born and raised. But not the way you would
6. think. I'm from the north eastern edge of Long Island...
7. Port Jeff. A nice little town... at least it *was* a nice little
8. town until everybody moved there from the city. What's
9. important about that is that I am not really a city type guy.
10. Port Jeff's a rural place. Lots of space to park your car and
11. not much crime... unless you count women cheating on
12. their husbands. Some people might call that a crime.

(Beat)

13. So, I'm not really a city type guy... although I live in the
14. city now. I should have made the move after nine eleven...
15. could of got a place downtown cheap. Everybody wanted
16. to get out downtown then... you could get a real good
17. deal... but that was then and this is now. The rent's are
18. so high now in Manhattan, I don't think I could afford
19. a crapper much less a studio apartment on a detective's
20. salary. So, I got myself a studio in Queens... actually
21. Flushing... ya'know they had the World's Fair there in
22. the sixties... they should really call it Flush it! At least my
23. building... something's always breaking down... ya'know
24. lights, leaky faucets, too much heat in the summer
25. not enough in the winter... like that. It's not that I'm
26. complaining the rent's cheaper than Manhattan... and

27. it doesn't take long to get to work. Just take the train.
28. Manhattan got too expensive... forget about it... nobody
29. can afford to live there... I think only Trump lives here
30. the rest of us are just visiting.

(Beat)

31. If you're wondering if I'm married... don't. It's a very
32. long story and I don't have it in me to tell it. Let's just
33. say... Yeah, I was married with the emphasis on was and
34. that married life just didn't go well with the job. And for
35. me... the job is all I got. That and a Plasma TV... that I still
36. haven't finished paying for.

(Beat)

37. Just got on duty, and was sitting at my desk getting ready
38. to do some follow up on a B and E that went down on 7th
39. Street. Nothing major, just trying check out a couple a
40. pawn shops... see if anything popped up. Most of the time,
41. these B and E's are addicts trying to get their hands on
42. something to sell so they can score their next fix. As usual,
43. I had no witnesses except a few looky loos who didn't see
44. anything. I really didn't have much but felt compelled to
45. go through the motions and file the paper... and to make
46. matters worse... I was on this alone... I was as they say
47. between partners. I seem to go through them like most
48. people go through underwear. No particular break up
49. issues come to mind... just that for one reason or another,
50. I've lost partners to transfers, the fire department, back
51. problems... the latest is maternity leave. It's not that I'm
52. anti female... but here it is... women want the job... then
53. they get pregnant and then they can't work the job. Not
54. only can they not work the job... but they can't be replaced.

55.   They're taking up space without even being here! So, I'm
56.   working alone... at least for now anyway.

(Beat)

57.   I was getting on the phone just about to get a make on a
58.   vehicle from a partial licence plate... Dealing with Albany
59.   is always a chore. When the robbery came down, a looky
60.   loo neighbor saw a blue vehicle drive away from the
61.   scene... only they didn't know the make and only got a
62.   part of its plate number.
63.
64.   I thought about doing it on the computer system but on
65.   this morning the system was extremely slow... like it is
66.   every other morning... But, look at it on the bright side...
67.   at least it hasn't crashed yet.

(Beat)

68.   Right behind me a uniform sergeant is trying to complete
69.   the initial processing of three male suspects who tried to
70.   snuff out one another with broken glass bottles the night
71.   before. When they brought em in... they were so hopped
72.   up on crack to do anything. On this morning... they were
73.   slowly returning to earth and not very happy campers. One
74.   of them in the holding cell was screaming at the top of his
75.   lungs that he wanted to press charges against the other
76.   for assault and the second one (with the satanic symbols
77.   tattooed all over his body) came down extremely hard and
78.   wouldn't let anybody touch him... to complicate it further,
79.   the third, with a purple mohawk is only 17-years-old and
80.   estranged from his family... so Social Services needs to be
81.   brought in for an appropriate adult'... so as usual, it's a
82.   fucking circus and I'm thinking to myself Why am I here?

(Beat)

83. That's when I get this call from an old high school buddy
84. Joey Taglio... a foreman on a renovation job on an old
85. turn of the century building down on Mulberry Street.
86. Says something about knocking out all the walls to make
87. lofts... and finding an old diary... and how he's got to get
88. the job done ASAP... and could I come over and bless it.
89. I thought to myself Why is calling me? I mean I see this
90. guy from time to time... have a few beers and a trip down
91. memory lane... but that's bout it. I'm about to ask him:
92. Why are you breaking my balls for this? Then he tells me
93. it's not just a book, there's a skeleton.

94. Okay... a skeleton... it's not a body... but it's close enough.
95. I said: Be right there! Thought to myself, definitely a
96. cold case... not an emergency... but at this moment, I'd
97. do anything to get away from this madhouse! I grabbed
98. my jacket and headed for the door. Just as I was almost
99. out, someone yelled out that the computer system had
100. just crashed but I pretended not to hear them. Once I was
101. out the door I just kept on going.

#32 ISABELLA ALESSO –
January 18, 1937 - MORNING (FEMALE)

(Period 30'S – New York Dialect)

1. Don't know what time it is. But I just can't sleep. My
2. father's pocket watch is on the dresser next to his bed...
3. but I'm afraid that I might wake him up. It's still dark, but
4. I know it's morning because the milk wagon just passed.

(Beat)

5. I'm usually the first one up and my job is start the stove
6. in da kitchen. That means putting some scrap wood into
7. the black stove and lightin it up. What a pain in the ass...
8. the wood sometimes is still damp and doesn't burn. We
9. don't have enough money for coal man so, every day after
10. school my older brothers Joey, Frankie and Vincenzo
11. have to go out and look for scrap wood. Vinnie hates to
12. look for wood and usually hides behind the horse barn on
13. Baxter street. The barn is a faded red building where all
14. the fruit peddlers and truckers keep their horses. I saw a
15. dead horse there once. Looked like he was sleepin on the
16. floor until you got up real close and see that his eyes were
17. open still. Didn't smell too good neither.

(Beat)

18. I didn't light the stove this morning because it was too
19. early and tip toed down the hall toward the roof stairway
20. past the bathroom. I couldn't see anything... but was happy
21. that it was empty. Most of the time it isn't. It's hard only
22. having one bathroom for five families on one floor but
23. after a while you get used to it. I found the stairway to the

24. roof and made my way up and could see a lot better once
25. I got to the top... lot's of light from the city. The mornin
26. air was cool and the only smell was from the fresh tar
27. patches that had been rolled over a hole Angelo Lazario
28. made when he made his pigeon cage. The hole caused a
29. leak when it rained... and they put tar all over it to fix it.
30. The black tar kinds of looks like licorice.

(Beat)

31. I looked down at the street from the rooftop. Ya' know...
32. this whole neighborhood is Italian. Everybody... for a while
33. I though that Johnny the Loopo (the baker's son) wasn't
34. Italian... everybody calls him "loopo botso" because he's
35. crazy. My mother told me once that he was from tenth
36. avenue before he moved here... so I just always thought
37. that he wasn't Italian. He hangs out his fire escape all day
38. collecting flies in a jar. One time a bunch of kids opened
39. the jar and let the flies out and Loopo Botso got real mad
40. and he hit one of the kids right in the kisser! The kid
41. didn't know what hit him and called Loopo Botso a crazy
42. assed Sicilian. It was then, that I realized Loopo Botso,
43. even though he was from way up 10th Avenue, was Italian
44. and that everybody, at least on this street, is from Italy.
45. If you go just two blocks though up to Mott Street it's
46. all Chinese. Some of my friends at school are Chinese.
47. Let's see there's Katerina Chang, and her brother Chin
48. or Chan... I don't know his name... but the Chinks never
49. come to Mulberry Street. Chinks is what my father calls
50. people from Chinatown.

(Beat)

51.   I'm gonna end here. I'll finish it tonight. I am so excited
52.   about Parent's Day. I have these red shoes with laces that
53.   tie right up to my ankles. I cleaned them up real good
54.   and I'll put on the dress I wear to church on Sunday. My
55.   father bought me those red shoes and I know he's going
56.   like that I have em on! I've just got to get there early to
57.   make sure every book in my desk in place, and clean the
58.   dark spots from my ink well. I want to be ready. I can't
59.   wait to see the expression on my father's face when he
60   walks through the door, I just can't wait!

61.   Somebody is coming up the roof stairs. I hope it's not my
62.   mother... then I'm really gonna get it!

#33 DETECTIVE GREEN #2 (MALE)

(New York Dialect)

1. "Hey Greeny, how's it going?" He used to call me Greeny
2. in high school and the name stuck. Joey Taglio, with
3. a large belly and hard hat, looked a lot older than I
4. remembered. I don't know why? I guess some people
5. age faster than others. I'm not saying that he looked like
6. my father or anything. But he got old. The one thing I
7. remember about him was that he liked malt beer. He used
8. to take me in his car, a 1960 Chevy Impala white with red
9. leather interior and a fox tail attached to the top of his
10. radio antenna. It's funny the details you remember.

(Beat)

11. He had a license and I didn't and we'd drive down to this
12. parking lot behind some trees off of the 25A to drink the
13. stuff. I hated it. I would never say that though. I drank
14. it like everybody else and threw up like everybody else.
15. I guess it was just something you had to go through in
16. high school like taking Geometry and English. Taglio got
17. so drunk one night that he slammed his Chevy into the
18. side of the International House of Pancakes on Route
19. 110. We could see the people laughing at him inside the
20. place That made him mad and he dropped his pants and
21. pressed his ass against the window. He called it a pressed
22. ham. After high school, he went to college somewhere
23. upstate and I got drafted and went to Nam. The rest is
24. history.

(Beat)

25. Joey walked me through a darkened scaffolded hallway
26. which lead up to a construction elevator. I couldn't help
27. but notice that this building, although it had seen better
28. days, had the remnants of a once elegant marble entry
29. way, and tile floor. All that was left that elegance was a
30. graffiti covered plaque that read 1902. On the way up,
31. Joey told me how they were converting this old brick shit
32. house to lofts for the what he called *shi shi ca ca* crowd
33. and that when he was done each unit would go for over a
34. thousand a square foot.

35. When we got to the top floor, I walked off the elevator and
36. took a short flight of steps to the roof. Joey looked at me
37. and said: There it is... It was about a six foot hole in the
38. tar roof underneath what looked like an old pigeon cage.
39. There was a space between the ceiling below and the roof
40. that had been covered up with tar more than once. A space
41. between then and now that time had forgot. Joey Taglio
42. took his hard hat off and said "Greeny you gotta help me
43. out here. This friggin skeleton is going to fuck up my
44. schedule. I gotta get a piece of paper that says I don't have
45. to stop my crew. So take a look and sign off on this." I took
46. the look. There was a child's skeleton... face down. Time
47. normally strips away the details but the tar sealed the space
48. like a cacoon. There were bits of a black cotton material.
49. Maybe a dress, mostly rotted away and the strangest thing,
50. one red shoe with laces... looked female. There was also
51. the tattered book which they found by its side. Its pages
52. were fused together in a cover of dried cracked tar. Joey
53. said: "So what`ya think?" Somebody fell... an accident. I
54. gently pulled away a portion of the tar revealing the back
55. of the skull. Two holes at the back portion of the skull
56. indicating blunt force trauma. Trauma caused by a large
57. object. Maybe a hammer? Usually you get typical signs: a

58. lacerated aorta or other major vessel, lacerated organ,
59. hematoma, contusions, crushed or severed spinal cord.
60. But, I didn't have anything like that here. All I have is a
61. skeleton. But I did know, this was not kind of injury you get
62. from a fall. Joey Taglio had stumbled into a homicide.

(Beat)

63. Joey looked at me waiting for an answer I knew I couldn't
64. help him as I flipped open my cell phone and called the
65. Crime Scene Investigation Unit. "Sorry Joey, I'm gonna
66. need some time on this." He pressed up close to me like he
67. did when we used to drink malts back in the parking lot.
68. "Greeny, cut me some slack on this. Just sign off on it and
69. let me finish this friggin job. I gotta a schedule to keep."
70. All at once I was back in Long Island sitting in his car
71. cruising Route 110. Back then he was the man but now
72. somehow it had all gotten old, even grotesque. "Joey, I
73. got a homicide here. I need a little time. Fuck you! You
74. flat-footed ass hole! That's what I get for calling a friend!"
75. He walked off and slammed the elevator door closed.
76. He called me his friend. No one had done that in a long
77. time.

(Beat)

78. I sat alone on the roof waiting for CSU. I know I wasn't
79. supposed to tamper with any of the evidence... but I found
80. myself gently peeling away the tar that sealed the book
81. until finally it opened. Its handwritten pages were stuck
82. together and needed delicate prodding and with a little
83. effort, I peeled open the first page and could make out
84. the writing it contained.

(Beat)

85. My diary 1937 Isabella Alesso age 15. I knew this diary
86. belonged to my skeleton. It was quiet on the roof. Not
87. much noise for the city, except the pigeons and delivery
88. trucks driving down the block and above you can see the
89. sky and a clear shot of the Empire State Building!

90. I wondered who Isabella Alesso was... and how she had
91. died in this place

#34 STARLET KONG - 1933 (FEMALE)

(New York Uptown Dialect)
(Sitting holding Telegram)

1. Hello darling. Just received this telegram all the way
2. from Hollywood, California from my good friend Mister
3. Google Barnes Jr. Just spent the weekend with him at one
4. of the most exquisite mansions on Long Island. Might
5. have been the Vanderbilt's. Actually, I don't remember.
6. What I mean to say is I have no specific recollection. It
7. was too dark when we drove out there and I had a bit too
8. much gin. (Laughs...) Boo Ha Ha.

(Beat)

9. Really, now that I think of it, it might not have been
10. Long Island after all. All I can remember was that the
11. roads were extremely long with no lights and any place
12. that far out of the city was Long Island. Googly said to
13. me: "Doll Face let's take a ride." I really think the reason
14. was that the speak easy we frequent was raided by the
15. police and Googly was taken back by the whole dreadful
16. situation. "We'd better lay it low and go someplace new."
17. So, that's exactly what we did and after a few Gin and
18. Tonics my head was spinning and I felt like I was wearing
19. an Easter bonnet only I wasn't... (laugh) "BOO HA HA
20. HA." Then Googly says "Let's toast my Hollywood trip!"
21. I ask, Hollywood, California? "Yeah, where all the movie
22. stars live. That's the one. I'm on the Limited, first thing in
23. the morning, out to Hollywood to produce a new motion
24. picture at RKO. It's called King Kong something or other
25. about a large ape captured from the wilds and brought to
26. Gotham?"

27. "Googly darling... this is just another one of your practical
28. jokes. (laughs) BOO HA HA HA! You're such a gadfly!
29. Am I right?

30. But he didn't say anything other than Let's drink to King
31. Kong! In short, King Kong although it sounded ridiculous,
32. was not a practical joke. Later that same night, we had my
33. chauffeur Charles drive us to Grand Central so we could
34. put Googly onto the train.

35. When we got there, Googly could hardly stand or talk,
36. I assume a bit too much gin. But, just before he passed
37. out, he told me he wanted me to join him in beautiful
38. Hollywood and audition for the lead in the film! I was
39. delighted! But before I could say yes, poor Googly passed
40. out. Charles and a very helpful Negro porter put him
41. on the train. It was awful not being able to say goodbye
42. properly and more importantly I couldn't stop thinking
43. about playing a part in King Kong!

(Beat)

44. Charles and I watched as the train pulled out of the station
45. on its way to Hollywood, California and that would be the
46. end of my story. But, not a word from Googly in more
47. than six months. I telegraphed him several times. But
48. alas, nothing. How dreadful.

49. That is until today. (Beat, opens the telegram and reads)
50. **Doll Face STOP On my way back to the apple STOP arrive**
51. **tomorrow STOP King Kong still a go STOP Can I stay at**
52. **your place STOP Googly**

53. How wonderful! But I'm a bit nervous. King Kong? Not
54. a very a catchy title. I like pictures with music in them
55. myself. Now give me the Jazz Singer. Now *that's* a picture.
56. But this ape movie is intriguing. I can picture it now.

57. The movie theater darkens and there I am on some
58. tropical shore. Then, sound of distant drums and endless
59. sea we see a title card from an Old Arabian Proverb: And
60. the Prophet said, 'And lo, the beast looked upon the face
61. of beauty. And it stayed its hand from killing. And from
62. that day, it was as one dead...

(Beat)

63. Really, now. How wonderfully exciting! (LAUGHS) BOO
64. HA HA HA.

(Exits)

#35 SPACE 3 (FEMALE)

(Enter slightly out of breath.)

1. Eww... Here we are... finally made it to the top! Welcome
2. to *Celestial Hills Cemetery and Water Park* in beautiful
3. sunny Southern California. Simply the ultimate place to
4. be when it comes to your final interment. (Long gaze
5. over a hillside) Now that's a view, pardon the pun, "to
6. die for". If you took away the smog and office buildings,
7. you could probably see clear across San Fernando Valley.
8. Magnificent, isn't it? Now, the actual space we discussed
9. is the western slope and will only have a canyon view. Not
10. as desirable as a city view, but *still* a view... and don't let
11. that steep forty five degree hillside slope bother you. Any
12. inconvenience made by the slope is more than adequately
13. compensated by this exclusive location. Make no bones
14. about it... when it comes to cemetery plots, I've got three
15. words for you... Location... Location... Location... We're
16. talking a prime location that you will want to own as your
17. special gateway to eternity. The market value on this
18. exclusive space can only rise with the passage of time...
19. and the Tahitian Mist landscaping makes you feel almost
20. like being on vacation! This exquisite parcel, worth well
21. over $4,000, can be purchased today for $3,500 plus
22. $100 for Transfer of Title. This is a once in a life time
23. opportunity for you to get in on the bottom floor. Also,
24. you can spare your children this expense and worry in
25. their time of grief. And you won't be alone. I don't want
26. to be a name dropper, but this parcel is adjacent to many
27. famous celebrities too numerous to mention. You can
28. truly spend eternity among the stars! Right this way. Please
29. watch your step. You can kill yourself trying to walk over
30. these grave stones.

#36 HELP WANTED, WE'RE DESPERATE (FEMALE)

(Holding News Paper and Cell Phone)

1. I thought I'd get a part time job... you know something
2. to get me some pocket money while I'm in school. So, I
3. checked out the Classified Section of the newspaper. Let
4. me tell you., pretty slim pickings... packers, deliverers,
5. store clerks and lots of accountants. Then I saw this ad
6. which read HELP WANTED WE'RE DESPERATE. I said
7. okay, what's the catch? *What* do they need help with and
8. *why* are they so desperate? I read further down the page
9. and all I could find was the phone number. 8 0 0 - 2 5 6
10. - 7667. That was it?

11. It was an 800-toll free number so it had to be some sort of
12. scam where they somehow get money out of you before
13. telling you anything or even worse you could automatically
14. be transferred to a toll charge number and be billed two
15. dollars per minute while they put you on hold and before
16. you know it your rack up twenty dollars on your phone
17. bill. Definitely some sort of rip off or worse, maybe it was
18. alien beings looking for people to experiment on! They
19. get you on the phone and ask you all sorts of questions
20. while they use superior technology to locate you. They
21. find you then abduct you and dissect your body!

(Beat)

22. But, then I thought, What the hell? I need a job, so I
23. picked up the phone and started dialing. I punched out
24. each number one, eight, zero, zero... and then I got
25. to the number two and stopped. I started looking at the

26. letters which corresponded to the numbers I was dialing.
27. What did they spell? That might give me a clue as to who I
28. was calling. 1 8 0 0 C, L, N, P, O, O, P? One eight hundred
29. clean poop? Aha! Now I knew why they were desperate!
30. Clean Poop! They're Crap Cleaners!

31. Whew, glad I checked. I mean how many people want to
32. do a job like that? The only way you could get somebody
33. to do that is to trick them with a stupid advertisement
34. Help Wanted We're Desperate. I mean what kind of idiot
35. would fall for bait like that?

(Beat)

36. But then again, I might have been wrong. So, I checked
37. the letters again to see if they might spell something
38. else. 1 8 0 0 - C, L, O, R, N, N, S... Cloe... Runs... Cloe
39. Run? Clones? Clones! This is some high tech company
40. creating clones! They're after my DNA! They're making
41. clones out of innocent people... but for what purpose? I
42. wouldn't mind more than one of me, but they probably
43. want to take blood... and that means needles! You tell
44. me, how many people like to get their bodies pricked by
45. needles? Of course they're desperate. How clever, how
46. very clever.

(Beat, then relaxed)

47. Am I'm just being paranoid? I mean, it's just a job, what
48. am I getting all worked up for?

(Then dialing)

49. One... eight... zero... zero... two... five... six... seven... six...
50. six... seven.... It's ringing. (starts looking at the letters
51. again) 1 800 - B, L, O, S... , M, O, R... BLOWS MORE!
52. Wait, it's a phone sex line! Of course, why didn't I see this
53. before! It's always boils down to sex.

(Into phone)

54. Hello? Yes, I called regarding your *disgusting* ad! How
55. dare you!

(Hangs Up)

56. Those degenerate bastards! No wonder there's so many
57. people unemployed!

(Puts newspaper under arm and exits.)

#37 DONUTS (MALE)

(Enter carrying a donut)

1. You know what they say? You are what you eat. And eating
2. one of these babies has got to be bad for you. You pop it
3. in your mouth and swallow it down real fast because you
4. can't wait to get to shove the next piece down your throat
5. and you don't want anyone to see you eat it because of the
6. big "G" Guilt. You feel guilty for eating it. You feel guilty
7. because everyone says it's bad for your body and you feel
8. guilty because you think of all the starving people in Africa
9. who eat less calories in a month then you're holding in
10. your hand.

(Takes a bite)

11. So you eat it fast…. you gulp it down without really chewing
12. fully and then it goes from your mouth down your gullet
13. to your stomach where it's processed and shipped directly
14. to your ass… where it's stored. That's why, when they say
15. **you are what you eat,** you know what I say about what
16. they say? Get a life! You bunch of pencil thin, politically
17. correct, schizophrenic, up tight carrot eating pain in the
18. asses! Get a fricken life! That's what I'd *like* to say. But,
19. you know what I do instead?

(Takes a bite.)

20. I gulp.

(**Exit walks off and hands the rest donut to a passerby.**)

#38 A CRIMINAL MIND (MALE)

(Enter - handed a donut from a passerby)

1.   Thank you... But I can't eat this ...

(Beat)

2.   Get a life? (Yells after him) Why don't **you** get a life?

(Gently puts it down on the ground like a planted flower)

3.   I'm doing my part for the environment. You know,
4.   feeding the ants. Ants are an essential part of the food
5.   chain. They eat the donut, the crickets and wasps eat the
6.   ants, the birds eat the crickets and wasps, the cats eat the
7.   birds... .and the dogs eat the cats. No that's not right...
8.   dogs don't eat cats. Dogs *chase* cats, but they don't eat
9.   them if they catch them. They just beat the crap out them
10.   and then let them go. All right, the truth is, I can't eat a
11.   donut... and it's not because of calories. Nothing like that.
12.   It's far more sinister. You see, a donut for me awakens an
13.   irresistible urge that I have deep inside of me. I suffer
14.   from having a criminal mind. It's that part of me that's
15.   impulsive and knows no rules. That dark part of me that
16.   wants it all now! When it sees something it wants, it just
17.   takes it! It lives deep within me and constantly struggles to
18.   be free to do as it pleases... and I do all that I can to keep
19.   my criminal mind in check. That's why I have a problem
20.   with this donut.

(Beat, then quietly)

21. This donut is a reminder of my past criminal life. You
22. see, when I was a small child, maybe five or six, I was a
23. thief... I stole not because I needed. I stole to fill the
24. lustful appetite of my dark criminal side. I was a thief at
25. one time in my life.

26. I stole... donuts. My cousin Johnny and I would wait
27. for the Dugan man. That was a baker in a truck that
28. would deliver hot steaming fresh from the oven cakes
29. and cookies right to your door every weekday morning
30. about eight o'clock... and the Dugan man, all dressed
31. in a clean white sharply pressed uniform that looked a
32. lot like the one the milk man wore, would roll up to my
33. cousin Johnny's house and knock on the door. My aunt
34. Viv, who spent most of her adult life with her hands under
35. running water washing just one dish at the kitchen sink,
36. would take and average of ten minutes to finish rinsing,
37. dry her hands and finally answer the door. When she
38. opened the door, she always had a surprised look on
39. her face: "What is it? Like she'd never seen him before.
40. The Dugan Man would say: Dugan Man! All right... all
41. right... let me see what you've got. Then she would scour
42. his packages of goodies and pick out a loaf of bread and
43. maybe a pie then go back inside to get her purse. As I
44. said, this process would take all of ten minutes.... that's
45. Six hundred seconds. A lot can happen in that amount
46. of time. It was a very sweet deal. The Dugan Man would
47. leave the back door of his truck wide open revealing a
48. virtual smorgasbord of baked delights. Now, we watched
49. this ritual every day and figured that we could get in the
50. truck, grab some donuts and be gone before the Dugan
51. man could make it back... and you know what? It worked
52. like a charm. Day after day we popped into the back his
53. truck and made out with a box of plain donuts. But

54. we didn't stop at that, after the plain, the next day we
55. worked our way up to white powered and each day up the
56. culinary ladder: sugar cinnamon, caramel, sugar glazed,
57. strawberry jelly, eclair and then *finally* chocolate. We made
58. out like bandits! A very sweet deal! (Beat) Then, about
59. half way through the summer, on one hot morning the
60. Dugan Man didn't show. We waited for him the next day
61. and the next... nothing. Then, I started thinking maybe
62. he got busted because we took all those donuts... maybe
63. he had to make good for them and maybe he lost his job
64. and *maybe* he had a wife and a bunch of starving kids to
65. feed and now he didn't have a job anymore and how we
66. were the cause of it all.

67. We were criminals, just like Al Capone and Lucky Luciano,
68. on our way to a life of crime. I couldn't sleep at night and
69. I told my cousin Johnny we had to come clean... confess
70. and make it all right again. He looked at me and said:
71. Confess? "You chicken shit, stool pigeon. You talk and
72. you're dead... D E D." So, what could I do? My cousin was
73. pretty big and I saw him kill a preying mantis one time...
74. took its head right off with his bare hands. So, I kept my
75. trap shut ... I held it in. I repressed it and it stayed with
76. me to this very day. I often think about trying to find
77. the Dugan Man., wherever he is, and set things right. Ya'
78. know, try to make him understand that I was just a kid.

(Beat)

79. Who am I kidding? The guy's probably pushing daisies by
80. now. But, if I could talk to him, I think he'd understand.
81. Now, I'm an adult, I know better and I'm not afraid of my
82. cousin Johnny any more. Besides he's doing a dime up in
83. Attica and can't touch me.

(Beat)

84.   So, that's why I can't eat a donut... when I see one, I get
85.   that urge. It's the dark side calling me back again. So, I
86.   just can't do it. Got to keep my criminal mind in check. I
87.   do it for myself.

(Beat)

88   and more importantly, I do it for the Dugan man.

(EXIT)

#39 EARLY BIRD SPECIAL (FEMALE)

1. On my way to the office, every morning, I walk past this
2. sign hanging in this arty Café type coffee shop which reads
3. EARLY BIRD SPECIAL - BUY ONE ENTREE AND GET A
4. SECOND OF EQUAL OR LESSER VALUE FREE. Pretty
5. good deal, I thought to myself. But, I never stop to check
6. it out. I just walk by the sign every day and really never
7. think much about ever going inside. It's just one of those
8. places you pass by but never stop at. Why? I'm not really
9. sure... maybe because I've never seen anybody sitting in
10. there. Maybe because the look of the place was neither a
11. café nor a coffee shop. I think that's what bothered me
12. the most. It's really stressful when you go into a place
13. and you really are not quite sure *where* exactly you are.

14. I just don't like when things are combined like those Swiss
15. Army knives that are also pocket watches, compasses, can
16. openers and nail clippers. Way too stressful for me to
17. carry all that responsibility of having to remember how
18. each part works and how to exactly get at it when you
19. need it. I've got one word for that... stressful.

(Beat)

20. Another thing, as I read the sign Early Bird Special, there
21. just isn't enough information. The sign doesn't indicate
22. any specific time which they define as early? More
23. importantly, why do you have to be early? Why don't they
24. ever have a late bird special? Why is early better than late
25. and what do they give you if you are early? Do you have
26. to be the first one in the door? What if I'm thirty seconds
27. late? Am I no longer considered an early bird? Does the
28. *intent* of being an early bird count? If you *try* to be early

29.   and you somehow fail at that endeavor, does that mean
30.   that the early bird offer gets rescinded? And there's the
31.   SMALL PRINT buy one entree and get a second of equal
32.   or lesser value free Who's going to do the math on that?

33.   Am I going to have to comb through the menu and settle
34.   for some hash plate to use as my second one free? And
35.   really, do you really think you'll get a second entree free?
36.   A second what? Try to figure that out. I just have one word
37.   for you. You got it, stressful. Who needs it?! I mean, the
38.   damn place can't even make up its mind whether it's a
39.   café or a coffee shop and *they* have the audacity to pass
40.   judgement on *you* by arbitrarily determining whether
41.   you're early or not!

(Beat)

42.   WHAT A LOAD OF CRAP! What the hell happened to just
43.   being on time.? Doesn't that count anymore? Couldn't
44.   there be an on time special to reward those responsible
45.   individuals who take the initiative to show up on time?
46.   What about them? Early Bird Special? What a crock! I
47.   just can't stand it when they try to take advantage of you!
48.   Those Bastards!

(EXIT)

#40 COFFEE PEOPLE (MALE)

(Holding cup of coffee)

1. Tough day eh? Me too? That's why I stopped off for a little
2. pick me upon the way here. Helps me put on the edge.
3. No, not drugs! (Takes a sip). I'm talking about a cup of
4. coffee, rich, dark, full bodied... warms me up all over.
5. (SIP) Nothing like it... There are two kinds of people in
6. the world. Tea People and Coffee People. Tea People are
7. usually left wing tree hugging Green Peacers that think by
8. drinking their decaf chai mint tea espressos that they're
9. saving the planet. They tell you that Coffee People are
10. hopped up caffeine freaks that don't have a clue about
11. the world. They will get on their tea box and preach to
12. you that coffee people have no idea where coffee comes
13. from and that millions of poverty stricken people in third
14. world countries work long hours growing and picking
15. coffee earning as little as a penny per pound. They look at
16. you smugly and say "How can you drink that cup of coffee
17. obtained by exploitation of the masses?" Those are the
18. Tea People.

(Beat)

19. I'm in the second group, the Coffee People. While we are
20. aware of the socioeconomic and political conditions on
21. the planet, we are not consumed them. To us, Coffee is
22. not just a drink... It's an experience that represents the
23. passage of time with friends or loved ones... a physical
24. state of being and more importantly a philosophy
25. of life. Yes, it's true to be a coffee person is to know
26. extreme ecstasy that can be found when you take your
27. first morning whiff of a full bodied, earthy and dark and

28. ferociously brewed cup of morning coffee. From that
29. first sip you are transported on a mystical journey to the
30. rustic rain drenched mountains of the old country where
31. Juan Valdez (his head covered by a sombrero so as to not
32. get too much sun) carefully hand picks each Columbian
33. bean and places it gently in a hemp sack strapped to the
34. back of his loyal donkey.

35. I've seen his picture on the can of coffee. Valdez doesn't
36. look exploited to me? In fact, he seems pretty damn
37. happy... and don't I deserve a little bit of happiness?
38. So, I take another sip... it's perfect.... and at that very
39. moment in time, there is nothing else in the universe
40. except me and my cup of coffee. This is life at its fullest
41. and the world is bright and full of possibilities.

(Beat, Drinks from Cup)

42. As you drink, you feel it rushing through your veins...
43. empowering you... bringing clarity where there was
44. none...
45. priming you like a pump...
46. winding you tighter and tighter
47. you're almost there... a pulsating
48. throbbing ball of energy...
49. ready to explode off the launch pad
50. like a rocket blasting off to the moon!!

(Gulps the remainder of the Cup Down, Then Calmly)

51. Now...
52. I'm ready to face the day.

(EXITS)

#41 ONE ON ONE (MALE)

(Folding a Sheet of Paper, then tapping a pencil)

1. Thank you for taking the time to talk to me. I wanted
2. to wait until the end of the day after everyone had gone
3. home to talk to you face to face rather than you hear things
4. from other people. Look I don't want to beat around
5. the bush. It's no secret that you haven't been happy here
6. since Michael Foster left. I also know that you had a more
7. than passing interest in applying for the Vice President
8. position that I now hold. Now, you know as well as I
9. that I had absolutely nothing to do with management's
10. decision not to give you the position and furthermore, at
11. the time the decision was made, I was not an employee of
12. this firm.

(Tapping Pencil Like a Drum, then Stops)

13. I also am keenly aware that when I came here more than
14. six months ago, that you were of the opinion that you
15. knew much more about running this division than I did.
16. I will agree that it has taken me several months to learn
17. the lay of the land here and become familiar with the
18. policies of the company. With that said, I am now more
19. comfortable with myself making decisions that I feel will
20. facilitate the smooth operation of this area.

(Beat, Read Paper, Tap Pencil Like a Drum, Then Stop)

21. I find your numerous contacts to senior management
22. criticizing my effectiveness insubordinate. I know you can
23. explain most of these treacherous communications away
24. by stating that you have had previous relationships with

25. senior management before my arrival and therefore felt no
26. need to go through me when initiating communication.
27. However, I don't see it this way and have frankly grown
28. tired of these One on One conversations where I talk then
29. you talk and then afterwards nothing changes... and what
30. we're after is change. Change not for change's sake alone
31. but change to make this area operate more efficiently and
32. that is something that it is now apparent that I will not be
33. getting from you.

(Beat)

34. As you are aware, you are an "at will" employee and as
35. of this moment, your services with the company are now
36. terminated. Your system access and password are now
37. inactive. You will be escorted by Mr. Martel of Security to
38. Human Resources for an exit interview and surrender of
39. office keys and parking access card. Upon your willing and
40. successful completion of this process, I've recommended
41. an adequate termination bonus equal to two weeks salary.
42. Security will assist you in the removal of any allowable
43. personal items that you may have in your office prior to
44. your final departure from the premises.

(Beat, Tap Pencil Like a Drum – Big Finnish then stop)

45. All right then. I'm so very glad we had this one on one.
46. It's important to communicate with one another. That's
47. what separates us from animals.

(Beat)

48. Have a good day... as best as can be expected under these
49. circumstances... and best of luck to you in your future endeavors.

#42 INTELLIGENCE (FEMALE)

(Holding a Man's Shirt)

1.   Today's like most days. You have to multi task to just get
2.   by. I have a slight opening here... just enough for one
3.   color load then I'm off to my son's school for a teacher
4.   conference. On the way back, I'll stop at the cleaners...
5.   two suits and a dress that I am planning to wear to my
6.   sister's birthday party. This morning I got up at the crack
7.   of dawn so I could get a jump on things. Lot's of luck.
8.   I had to get the kids ready for school. For my daughter
9.   Jamie that meant putting out her school clothes on her
10. bed.... usually jeans and a top, socks and shoes... nothing
11. fancy. For a six-year old, she's pretty independent and
12. wants to dress herself. Now, my boy, Justin at seven, is
13. another story all together. No matter what I put out for
14. him, he'll want to wear the same thing everyday. I used to
15. fight it, but now have learned to go with the flow... and
16. just let him wear it. (Beat) This morning though wasn't too
17. bad, he wore the same pants as yesterday, but thankfully
18. wanted to wear his Batman shirt, which was clean. So, I
19. was home free at least for today and fed them fresh fruit
20. and cereal, packed them in the mini van and took off for
21. school without a hitch. I didn't get a chance to say much
22. to my husband, Robert. He got home late last night (had
23. to stay at the office) and was a little slow getting up this
24. morning. He normally leaves the same time we do and
25. heads for the train station where he catches the 6:45 for
26. the city ... and this morning was no different. Like most
27. days, no matter how much you try to plan, it somehow all
28. goes to hell. When I got to school this morning,

29. Justin's teacher Mr. Laslo said that he couldn't meet with
30. me then and it would be better if I could meet him later
31. in the morning. So... I agreed to meet him at 10:30 A.M.
32. So, I had some extra time and decided to come back
33. home. When I got home, I figured I had just enough
34. time to make the beds, clean up breakfast, take a shower
35. and do one load of color laundry. That was the plan... and
36. I was just getting started, gathering the colored clothes
37. when I saw Robert's shirt hanging on the chair next to the
38. bed and I thought; It's not in the hamper but I'll throw it
39. in anyway.

40. At first, when I picked it up, I didn't quite recognize the
41. smell … something like Gardenias… . the kind of odor
42. you smell when you're in Hawaii when you just get off the
43. plane. But then I thought. We don't live in Hawaii and I
44. placed the shirt up to my face and took a deep breath.

(She picks up the shirt, holds the shirt up to her face and smells it.)

45. Smells like Gardenia. But, not the flower... more like
46. "Gardenia" the perfume. No man would wear a smell so sweet.

(Beat)

47. So sweet... You have no idea the thoughts that went
48. through my mind as the sweet fragrance made its way
49. up my nose, into my lungs... I was assaulted by visual
50. images of Robert with another woman. He got home late
51. and had probably been out. But if he'd been out, why
52. would he so carelessly leave the evidence behind. Surely
53. he would know that I would discover it... or did he think
54. that I was so ridiculously stupid that I would not be able

55. to put the facts together? Did he think that my brain was
56. limited only to those menial functions as cleaning and
57. feeding? Could he be so arrogant as to think that? At that
58. moment, I was angry because it was a double blow... one
59. that he had cheated on me and secondly that he thought
60. that I was so stupid that I wouldn't even discover it? THAT
61. BASTARD! I WILL POISON HIM, CUT UP HIS DEAD
62. BODY AND BURY IT IN THE DESERT!

(Beat)

63. My anger then lead to clarity... one word came to my
64. mind. INTELLIGENCE. I was thinking of the full
65. spectrum of its meaning. The capacity to acquire and
66. apply knowledge... the facility of thought and reason...
67. and more importantly the superior use of the powers of
68. the mind. My first step was to investigate further. Perhaps
69. a trip to the city - outside Robert's office, to observe and
70. collect data. Secondly, develop a comprehensive strategy
71. and lastly to execute that strategy... and bury the bastard.

(Beat)

72. So... I won't be washing this shirt today. Instead I will
73. put it in a safe place... off site, have it analyzed and used
74. as evidence. I must remain calm and conduct additional
75. intelligence... gather additional data... while retaining
76. my normal routine. I have just enough time to make the
77. beds, clean up breakfast, take a shower and do one load
78. of color laundry.

(Beat)

79. Then, get ready for my 10:30 with Mr. Laslo...

#43 EXPLORING WHITENESS (FEMALE)

(Observing a painting, then a sigh of wonderment)

1. I think that out of all of my five senses, my strongest
2. sense is visual. I respond to almost everything visually. For
3. example, I just love looking at paintings.

(Looks)

4. Beautiful! It's called A SUMMER's DAY and the artist has
5. created the mood and feeling of the work by using daring
6. brush strokes of color! You are literally assaulted by the
7. interaction of blues, greens... yellows... and occasional
8. splotches of red. Ab... so... lute... lee... gorgeous!

9. Now with that said, I will also say that I don't automatically
10. fall in love with every painting I see.

(Beat)

11. About a year ago I had met a friend at the Palace Hotel for
12. lunch and when I got out it was raining cats and dogs and
13. I couldn't get a cab. So I started to walk up a few blocks
14. and cross over to 6th when I found myself in the middle of
15. a down poor on 53rd. So, I decided to wait in the lobby of
16. Museum of Modern Art until the rain slowed down. When
17. I got inside, I was confronted with a large sign which read
18. EXPLORING WHITENESS. The museum attendant said
19. it was a must see exhibit. I paid the entry fee and made my
20. way up the escalator toward the main gallery and a slightly
21. smaller sign which read plainly EXPLORING WHITENESS
22. - THIS WAY. As I passed through a grand entry way into
23. the gallery, I wasn't quite sure if what I was looking at.

(BEAT)

24. It was one large gallery in which there was one long row of
25. multiple sized blank canvases. Each canvass was a slightly
26. different shade of white... ergo the title exploring... you
27. know what... whiteness. I slowly walked down one side
28. of the gallery slowly, passing a line of blank canvasses
29. thinking to myself... this must be a mistake.

30. Then I came to one large blank canvass and next to me
31. there was a rather tall gentleman who held his chin while
32. staring intently into the large blank space as if he could
33. see something extraordinary and I couldn't.

34. I looked at him and looked at the blank canvass and wasn't
35. quite sure if he was real or part of the exhibit. He finally
36. came to life and looked at me. "Well... what do you think?"
37. I didn't know what to say. He filled in for me: "Amazing...
38. isn't it?" I answered: I suppose so, but there's nothing on
39. any of these canvasses. He beamed: "Exactly! That is what
40. is so brilliant about it! The artist is saying What if I gave
41. you NOTHING! What would you make with it?" I said:
42. What would I make with nothing..? Nothing? He thought
43. for a moment and replied: "Yes, I suppose you could."
44. Then walked away.

(Beat)

45. As I said earlier, I'm a visual person, so I felt almost
46. abandoned without any visual stimulation. I thought I'd
47. be much better off out in the rain and headed for the
48. door, when I came face to face with the next exhibit -
49. BOX OF TIDE.

(Beat)

50. Now this was an exhibit I could sink my teeth into. Visual
51. with color and mass! And there it was on a blank platform...
52. a Box of Tide... you know one of those extra large boxes of
53. clothing detergent you buy at COSTO. There it was... just
54. sitting there on a platform with a bronze printed plaque
55. next to it which simply read BOX OF TIDE. I stood for
56. what must have been thirty seconds looking at it with my
57. right hand holding my chin

58. When finally I was interrupted by that same tall gentleman
59. I had seen before. He looked at me and said: "Well?"
60. and I smiled and said What if you were given a box of
61. Tide... just an empty box of Tide and nothing else...
62. what would you put in it? He thought for a while and said:
63. "Detergent?" I thought deeply for a moment and replied:
64. Yes... I suppose you could...

(EXIT)

#44 CUTS (MALE)

(Holding a newspaper)

1. A lot of people get *very confused* about the word Cuts. Not
2. me. It means less, reduction... trim back...   prune...
3. decrease... diminish or eliminate. You get the picture?
4. Everyday there's news about how we as a consumer or a
5. citizen are paying more for something and getting less.
6. It's everywhere... on TV, Newspapers... on billboards ...
7. . everywhere.

(BEAT)

8.   You don't need a college degree to figure out that cuts are
9.   NOT A GOOD THING. Unless, you don't know it's a cut?
10. So, here's what they do... they don't make a cut sound
11. like a cut. What they really want to do is confuse you ...
12. so when they do it... they always want to make it sound
13. like they're doing you a special favor... they couch their
14. message in words like in order to provide you with the
15. best service, our new improved ... now better than ever!
16. What they won't ever say is we're cutting! It's a cut. You're
17. getting less and paying more!
18. They think, if they told you the truth, you'd scream bloody
19. murder.

(Beat)

20. Maybe we would. Don't even think about complaining to
21. the government because they do it too!

22. Our elected officials promise everything when they're
23. running for office... but once they get elected,   they

24.   change: After careful analysis, and reviewing priorities
25.   versus resources, we're going to have to reallocate our
26.   energies to address the over budget line items... nothing
27.   is set yet... our limited staff will review the inconclusive
28.   data and make subsequent recommendations to the sub
29.   committee which in turn will debate the issue before
30.   making a final advisement to the full committee ... and
31.   in the interim we are suspending this service...

32.   They make it sound like they're doing you a favor, but in
33.   reality, it's a cut. "Why can't they just say I know I promised
34.   you more, but now that I'm in office., I've changed my
35.   mind. Or even better. Now that I'm elected, I'm cutting
36.   my salary and guess what? It won't cost you a dime!

(Beat)

37.   Hey wait a minute... that would also be a cut wouldn't it?
38.   That's still a cut... isn't it? Or is it?

(Beat)

39.   Now *I am* confused ...

(EXIT)

#45 X (MALE)

(Holding an extremely small paper shopping bag by its handle)

1. Just got out of the hair salon How do I look? First thing
2. I'm going to do is go home and wash this stinky gel out of
3. my hair and comb it the way I like it. They slick it back into
4. your hair with both hands and you look more like Elvis
5. than you want to and you make the fatal mistake by saying
6. "Wow… what's that? Smells nice." This opens the door
7. and they jump in: New product called X… You smile: Very
8. cool! and before you can say another word, they place a
9. mirror in your hand, spin the chair around and show you
10. the back of your head. You look with curiosity at the back
11. of your head and think. is that really what people see when
12. they walk behind me? Your stylist says: Is that all right…?
13. and you say something like… Beautiful, gorgeous… hot…
14. I can't believe it… it's fabulous! When actually, you really
15. don't care very much about what the back of your head
16. looks like… I mean it's not a priority, but you go with
17. the flow. They spin you back forward again, and in one
18. swift move, brush the loose hairs off you and snap off the
19. girly smock you've bee wearing. They give you the look as
20. they smile. The look means two things. One, you better
21. say one more time … it's a good job… and two… get the
22. fuck out of here, I've got another appointment waiting.
23. You're escorted to the reception area where they ask you
24. the big question: How are you on hair products today?
25. They say this while putting a new jar of X in your hand
26. as if to say you said you liked it? You didn't lie to me did
27. you? Now you feel so obligated to buy the shiny red jar of
28. smelly slick because you *did* say how great it smelled So,
29. you're screwed. I could use some gel. I think I'll take that

30.   jar of? The girl chewing the gum behind the cash register
31.   smiles and says: "*X*" Before you can say another word,
32.   the jar is in a bag and you've racked up another $25.00
33.   dollars onto your bill.

34.   They smile at you as if to say: You've made a quality
35.   choice for yourself and will live a better life for it. You
36.   sign the credit card receipt and add some cash for a tip
37.   and then BAM! Gear change. You get the hairdresser hug
38.   accompanied by the Bye love! and before you know it,
39.   you're out the door holding your bag of "*X*" and thinking
40.   to yourself I really can't walk around the street looking
41.   like this. I gotta get home and get this shit off of me and
42.   I mean now!

(Beat)

43.   And I mean now!

(EXIT)

#46 GOOD-BYE (MALE)

1. One thing that I just hate to do, is say the word Goodbye.
2. I don't like the good and bye put together in just that way.
3. There's such a finality to them. When you say goodbye
4. you're expressing first a parting and secondly an ending.
5. Now not all partings are endings. That's where I have the
6. problem. I don't like endings... endings of anything. I
7. like to think of life as a continuous series of events and
8. relationships that progress onward into infinity ... yes
9. they ebb and flow but they don't end. So when I leave
10. someone, I prefer to say See you later... or catch you
11. later. As if to say until next time ... so we're not done. In
12. fact, we may never be done. It doesn't have to end.

(Beat)

13. I like it better that way. I like to think of the infinite
14. possibilities of the universe both good and bad, none of
15. which have to end. Think about love ones, people that
16. you have known that have died, didn't you think about
17. the last moment you saw them alive? What you said? What
18. they said. How you parted? Ask yourself, did I say good
19. bye? Did I say anything?

(Beat)

20. Think about that next time you leave someone.

(Beat)

21. Catch you later.

(EXIT)

#47 CHICKEN (MALE)

1. *When I was sixth grade halfway between boy and man, I had*
2. *a friend in my class. His name was Chicken. That wasn't*
3. *his real name ... but the kids in the class used to call*
4. *him Chicken.*

5. *Chicken was a freckle faced, lanky stick of a kid with a*
6. *bush of red hair on top of his head. He had a hard time*
7. *fitting into his wooden desk because his legs were too*
8. *long. We used to say he had long chicken legs... but that's*
9. *not how he got the name Chicken ... and yeah ... he did*
10. *have a real name, Jacob Lucas. But no one except our*
11. *teacher Mr. Garvey ever called him Jacob. To us, he was*
12. *just Chicken.*

(Beat)

13. *Chicken came into our class about the middle of the school*
14. *year. Mr. Garvey brought him in to the class and said*
15. *something like Now boys and girls, I want you to say*
16. *hello to our new classmate who just moved here from West*
17. *Virginia.* Say *hello Jacob ! Nobody really knew where West*
18. *Virginia was as we sang out* H E L L O J A C O B. *Then,*
19. *Mr. Garvey continued:* Now Jacob, tell us something
20. about yourself. The poor kid looked like he was going to
21. pass out. *His face got redder than his hair and he started*
22. *sweating then he stood up tall like he was facing a firing*
23. *squad, took a deep breath and cleared his throat.* Jacob
24. Lucas... that's my Christian name after my dad ... and
25. my grandfather before him ... think the Lucas's came to
26. West Virginia from Ireland ... even thing one er two of
27. em scrapped with Indians in the French and Indian War.
28. *That was the first time I heard a West Virginia accent.*

29.   *He went on:* Jacob Lucas that what it sez on paepers
30.   an'all ... but I go by the name Chicken. My Dad started
31.   it cause he said I like to run so much ... Ya`know like a
32.   crazy chicken.   I got mad at first, but then, I kinda got
33.   used to it ... suppose Dad figured right that chicken was a
34.   fittin name to find out who yer friends ire ... and make ya
35.   tough enough to take care yer enemies ... if ya have anny.
36.   So, Jacob Lucas's my name ... and y'can call me that but
37.   everybody that's my friend ... calls me Chicken. Ya`know
38.   like the bird. *There were a few giggles followed by silence*
39.   *Chicken looked out over the room:* Any Questions? *Lucy*
40.   *Sullivan, pulled on one of her pigtails when she raised her*
41.   *hand:* What's West Virginia like?

(Beat)

42.   *Chicken thought for a moment then said:* If you could
43.   close yer eyes and imagine Heaven right here on this
44.   earth, I spect that's West Virginia. My Dad and I lived on
45.   this farm down Putnam County ways. Mom died was I was
46.   born ... never met her, so it was jest him en me. Our farm
47.   is between the railroad tracks and the river ... nothin to
48.   hollar at ... just a small patch a dirt and green. I went to
49.   Bunker Hill Schewl ... near the mines ... that is till Dad
50.   got sick with some kinda cancer. Then, I couldn't go to
51.   schewl much ... had to take care of the farm... weren't
52.   too bad ... that is till Dad got sicker and ... then he died.
53.   He's all I had... that and a second cousin ... living up
54.   here. *The room became still and Chicken looked over at*
55.   *Mr. Garvey to show him where he should sit. When Susan*
56.   *Sullivan sat up straight and said:* Tell us more. *Chicken*
57.   *hesitated:* Not too much more ta tell ... exceptin maybe
58.   the day my Dad died... I was cryin next ta him lyin in bed
59.   en all en dedn't want to be an orphan an I asked him

60. what was I goin ta do... He whispered in my ear. Son,
61. don't matter what'ya plant ... it's how ya plow the field
62. and make it grow. I never quite rightly knew what he did
63. mean... being that he passed right after he told me. Guess
64. I'll figure it'all out someday when I get older and such.
65. Seein as this my first day a school and all... I kinda thinka
66. ya'all as my freinds... and that bein so... and ya'll lettin
67. me jabber up here, I'll be yer friend as well ... for life.
68. So ya'll can call me Chicken!

(Beat)

69. *... and that's what we called him Chicken. Chicken went to*
70. *the same school as I did right through high school. He was*
71. *my best friend. Whenever I needed anything, Chicken was*
72. *always there. In our senior year, he was the top running*
73. *back on our school football team. I guess his father was*
74. *right... Chicken loved to run when he got the ball he*
75. *just took off and there wasn't much anybody could do to*
76. *stop him... scouted by all the colleges for a scholarship.*
77. *(BEAT) That was until he started to change. It was hardly*
78. *noticeable at first ... wasn't as fast as he used to be and*
79. *was tired all the time. Then, he got worse.*

(Beat)

80. *I remember the day he went to the hospital. We'll fight*
81. *and beat this! He looked me in the eye and said: We sure*
82. *will! But he didn't. (BEAT) Chicken died four months*
83. *later ... I wanted him to fight ... fight for his life but he*
84. *just wouldn't do it. He died. I lived . (BEAT) And for*
85. *a long time, I was very angry at Chicken ... for dying ...*
86. *and because he seemed to just accept his fate. He knew he*
87. *was going to die and he seemed so content with it. Some*

88. *people work their whole lives chasing their dreams and*
89. *when they get it, they're still not happy. He never even*
90. *had the chance.*

(Beat)

91 *Now that time has passed, I think I understand. He*
92. *savored every moment of it and fought to make what he*
93. *had the best life possible. He truly lived until the day he*
94. *died. No regrets. (BEAT) Chicken, now I understand.*
95. *Don't matter what `ya plant... it's how ya plow the field...*
96. *and make it grow.*

#48 NO SOUND TV (MALE)

(Walking deliberately in place, then stop)

1. I'm on the tread mill the other day at the gym taking a
2. brisk walk. Maybe three and half... four miles an hour
3. with an incline. There's not much to do but walk and
4. if you have a set of head phones, you can watch one of
5. the three TV sets they have hanging from the ceiling. I
6. brought a set of radio head phones so I could tune in
7. and hear the sound. It was okay, but radio head phones
8. were so uncool.... so clunky... they made me feel like I
9. was wearing a Mickey Mouse hat... and you don't want to
10. look like Mickey Mouse when you're working out at the
11. gym. So, I started walking without them ... at first it was
12. boring ... nothing to do. You keep looking down at the
13. timer and watch the seconds tick by... makes you feel like
14. you'll never get through it.   Then little by little, I started
15. watching the three TV's which I could see just fine...
16. but couldn't hear without the headphones. Most of the
17. time, they have them tuned in to all sports stations, music
18. videos or reality TV. But every once in a while they put on
19. a news station. That's when I watch the most. Because
20. news, believe it or not, is the most visual.

(Beat)

21. I mean, there are sub titles below the screens, but they are
22. usually thirty seconds behind the picture. So you see the
23. caption "Four dead today in the Middle East" appearing
24. under underneath a picture of a talking carrot. So totally
25. illogical that I almost fell off the tread mill a few times because
26. I was so concentrated on trying to figure out what was going
27. on, that I stopped walking and went flying backwards.

(Beat)

28. So, for my own safety, I started watching the gym TV's
29. without subtitles... . it's like going without a bra... . you
30. absolutely think you need it... and then... voila! No big
31. deal! And I will tell you, it's a freeing experience. Just
32. the picture... no sound... no subtitle... it's sets you free.
33. For example, take music videos... (**Gesture hand like a**
34. **gun**) You get all the sex and violence without struggling
35. to understand the lyrics... just what does yo yo yomean
36. anyway? And when they bump and grind, you can watch
37. it without trying to decipher what they're saying... just
38. think... bump... grind... without the hoochy mama
39. mama mama.

(Bump and grind in silence)

40. See what I mean?

(Bump and grind again, but slower)

41. What about reality shows? They really come to life without
42. sound... do you really care what they say to each other
43. in REAL WORLD? Let's face it, you just want to see
44. them walk around in their underwear and pseudo sexual
45. situations ... and let's not forget the Before and After
46. shows... Very visual.

(Beat)

47. Then you've got the news shows... most visual of all.
48. News people know they have to be visual or people will
49. change the channel and put on a game show. They go
50. out of their way to visualize everything. For example,

51. the weather reports use lots of little pictures of frowning
52. clouds and smiling sunshine. And when a reporter stands
53. outside in the one hundred twenty mile an hour winds
54. during a hurricane... . ever ask yourself why? It's visual!
55. Traffic reports... usually have pictures of little cars trying
56. to move down animated freeway arteries... if they crash
57. into one another that means there's an accident... not
58. as good as the hurricane... . but still it's visual. BANG!
59. BANG! BANG, as the little cars flash brightly on the
60. screen. You got to love that.

61. Even murders are shown visually. YOU SEE the chalk
62. outline where the victim has fallen... and for the artistically
63. inclined... YOU SEE hand rendered drawings of court
64. room proceedings... and perhaps the most visual of all...
65. there's the all time favorite (especially in California), the
66. FREEWAY CHASE! What can be more visual than that?
67. The alleged car thief drives a stolen vehicle on a minimum
68. of three freeways, cuts through private neighborhoods
69. and if possible side swipes several civilian vehicles along
70. the way... this real life action packed visual adventure
71. unfolds moment to moment as we watch from the sky cam
72. helicopters. Now **that's** visual entertainment! No sound...
73. No subtitles... Just the picture...

(Beat)

74. Now, I turn the sound off when I watch TV at home... I
75. can't help myself. Once you start, there's no turning back.
76. It's what I call No Sound TV...

(**Back to running in place, then exit**)

#49 THE MALL (FEMALE)

1.   It's an addiction... that can trigger at *any* ti..
2.   middle of the night or during the day . While y.
3.   walking on the street, driving in your car, at work, at a
4.   wedding, getting your teeth cleaned by a dental hygienist
5.   and then it strikes without warning! That irresistible urge
6.   you cannot resist pulsating from within you deeper and
7.   deeper till finally BAM! You lose control and HAVE to
8.   give in... You want to go to the mall.

(Beat)

9.   Mall? Did you say Mall? Sorry, anytime somebody says
10. Mall It triggers my addiction and I immediately want to
11. go there. No, it's more than that, I have an unrelenting
12. *desire* to go there. I mean I *really* want to go to the Mall
13. and I *really* have no idea why this happens. It just does.

(Beat)

14. You ever stop and think about what you do at the Mall?
15. Really not much... you walk around ... look at stuff ... buy
16. something on impulse... maybe eat something and then
17. what? You hang a bit more ... then go home. As soon as
18. you get home... you want to go again! You could do it
19. on a Monday... and want to do it again on a Tuesday...
20. even though you were just there? What's that all about?
21. (BEAT) I can only speak for myself. It's kind of a theory. I
22. mean, there's no research behind it... Here it is.

Why is that?

(Beat)

23. Going to the Mall addresses the human species primordial
24. instinct to hunt and gather. And what is going to the
25. Mall? Isn't it hunting and gathering? The Stone age man
26. foraged open fields and mountains for fruits and berries...
27. and when he could, he hunted Mastodons ... and other
28. fur bearing creatures... driven by instinct, desire and the
29. will to survive.

30. Doesn't that sound just like the Mall? Isn't the Mall a
31. modern day version of this ritualistic cleansing of our
32. innate desire to hunt and gather? We go to the Mall
33. and shop at Bloomingdales, Prada and Gucci to survive.
34. Just like a Stone Age quietly tracking the footprints
35. of a mastodon... we flip through a rack of clothing or
36. accessories... hunting for the perfect fit... and like the
37. Stone Age hunter whose heart races as he is about to make
38. the kill... our pulse races when we come face to face with
39. that one irresistible word that speaks to our hearts... You
40. know the word I'm talking about... the word SALE!

(Beat, CROUCH LOW)

41. Even as I speak the word... my instincts take over... my
42. body language changes. I'm no longer myself. I *am* that
43. Stone Age hunter poised to strike... 40% off ... 50%
44. off... POW! I strike! My credit card strikes the heart of
45. my prey like a spear! I don't need it... but I buy it anyway!
46. I can't help myself... I'm fighting thousands of years
47. of instinctual behavior... and once that credit card is
48. swiped and I see the word approved on the little screen,
49. I feel sated... good all over... the hunter has acquired
50. its prey.

(Beat)

51. But the bad part is.... it doesn't last long does it? As
52. soon as you ***do it...*** you want to ***do it*** again... you're blood
53. thirsty for more and the hunt starts all over again... you
54. just ***have*** to go to the mall...

(Beat)

55. Mall? Did you say Mall?

#50 CREATIVE HIDING (MALE)

(Holding a shoe)

1. At one point or another in your life, there will always
2. be one of those moments when you're going to have to
3. face up to something that you don't want to ... either
4. because it's too painful to experience... you're afraid of
5. the truth or you just plain don't want to get caught doing
6. something you're not supposed to be doing. We all do it
7. ... on purpose... or sometimes without even knowing we
8. do it. What I'm talking about is CREATIVE HIDING. It's
9. our way of not dealing and it occurs almost instinctively.
10. Here's how it works.

(Beat)

11. Your girlfriend says to you: We've been going out for six
12. months now and I really think it's time for us to take the
13. next step and make a commitment to one another.

(Beat)

14. The key word here is *commitment* which most guys fear
15. more than a dentist drilling a cavity. The word *commitment*
16. causes the brain to send alarm signals down to the rest of
17. the body.

(Beat – Alarm Sounds like a submarine diving – "umm umm umm")

18. Dive! Dive! Dive! Rig for Depth Charges! And it's exactly
19. what you do... you creatively hide and literally slip
20. beneath the waves of your emotional surface... just like a

21. submarine. Technically, what happens is, that you focus
22. your attention on an object . . any object... other than
23. the person you are talking to... for example, this shoe. As
24. soon as you hear the word commitment you focus on this
25. shoe... and maybe this lace become the most important
26. thing in your world.

(Hold up shoe close to your face)

27. You look at it closely ... you smell it ... you check the laces
28. for wear and tear... you investigate the soles for mileage,
29. you rub the scuff marks softly. In short, you give it all to
30. this shoe ... while she is talking about commitment.

31. This is creative hiding ... ergo hiding creatively. If you
32. could, you would beam up to the Enterprise... but you
33. can't! So you hide in the shoe or any other object that
34. you can grab at a moment's notice. You're probably
35. wondering... . when she says... . commitment and I'm
36. creatively hiding, what do I say back? Here it is...

(Look closely at the shoe)

37. I hear ya... But... Whoa... I think I better get some new
38. laces on this baby... looks like they're going to go soon...
39. better get on it right now.

(Beat)

40. Creative Hiding... Try it., works like a charm. Just don't
41. say you got it from me.

(EXIT)

#51 WELCOME TO THE JUNGLE (MALE)

1. Welcome to the jungle... that's the world we live in...
2. It's not like it used to be. In the old days when there was
3. honor among men Now, its dog eat dog... Ya`know what
4. I mean... the blunt realities of primitive life. But not in
5. the jungle... on the freeway, waiting on line at the super
6. market... walking out your front door to pick up the
7. morning paper. A jungle... where predators hunt prey
8. and if you haven't figured it out yet, *we* are the prey.

(Beat)

9. I read about this guy that got up one morning walked
10. down his driveway to pick up his newspaper... and before
11. he could stoop down to read the front page headline, a car
12. sped by and pumped three shots into his chest. I wonder
13. if he even knew what hit him... just bent down to pick up
14. the paper... and BAM BAM BAM.... BLACKOUT... or
15. maybe did he think to himself I should'a stayed in bed a
16. little later this morning. We'll never know the answer to
17. that question because he's dead and the ass hole that shot
18. him is living the life somewhere or maybe by now... he's
19. dead too... we'll never know the answer to that either
20. because he was never caught. Just another statistic.

(Beat)

21. In the jungle ... there's no good and bad. Only the strong
22. and the weak. Society creates good and bad... but now,
23. the badness is so random... it's badness without purpose.

24. I'm not saying that in the old days killing was better
25. because people were more civil and only killed with a
26. specific purpose... that would be bull shit. What I am
27. saying is the life of a human being has evolved into a cheap
28. commodity... a random entity which is used for marketing,
29. consumerism, war, or entertainment purposes.

30. And... as part of any of these, a human life can be
31. terminated and then calculated as a statistic then
32. forgotten. I am going to kill you now just because.... just
33. because I don't like your hat... just because you happen
34. to be walking there at that moment, just because I want
35. what you have... and I'll just take it... Just because I
36. feel like it... BAM! Your dead.... . you're number is up
37. and your life is not even worth the thought behind my
38. taking it.(BEAT) And when a life is taken in just this
39. way, we watch it on Television on the news or reenacted
40. as part of a drama, there is really not much difference
41. between the two... we are entertained as death is played
42. out on our digital TV screens live in crisp detail, dissected
43. and analyzed from every point of view. We reach for the
44. remote to turn it off... but can't. We have to watch... in
45. seeing the misery of others, we find a strange comfort. It
46. didn't happen to us. At least not this time ... We're still
47. alive! And if we're careful, we'll stay that way. Through
48. our television surround sound stereo speakers, the pulse
49. of the asphalt Serengeti goes on... predator and prey.

(Beat)

50. Like I said, Welcome to the jungle.

52 PICK UP EPILOGUE (FEMALE)

(A deck of 52 playing cards has fallen to the ground. Pick up the deck of cards one by one as you speak.)

1.   Time is an invisible spirit
2.   nestling up close beside us by just cause
3.   as a companion would on a journey to
4.   a destination impossible to see from where we stand
5.   and by wanting of its care
6.   we wear it like a caligraphic notation upon our sleeves
7.   calling attention to each letter and mark put upon there
8.   we require its presence at every moment
9.   consuming it without full measure
10. each sunrise through hurried day
11. and
12. in drunken moonlit nights
13. expending its glow
14. in whitened revelry
15. we dance
16. until the shadows of autumn
17. burn't like umber's gristle
18. drunken down
19. fade then
20. fall away
21. and darken the ground
22. marking each our step from beginning to end
23. not in parade
24. but in forgotten moments
25. each vanishing as they came
26. a stolen season
27. in want of repeat

(Pick up last card, then exit)

ADDENDUM #1
PERFORMANCE PRESENTATION

BREAKDOWN BY AGE AND GENDER

Cast of Six

Character #1 - YOUNG MALE (TEEN - TWENTIES)

#2	CONSERVATION
#7	CRIME
#12	GUYS LIKE STOOGES GIRLS LIKE LUCY
#20	BREAKING UP #1
#24	I WANT TO BE LIKE AN INDIAN
#37	DONUTS
#40	COFFEE PEOPLE
#46	GOODBYE
#50	CREATIVE HIDING

Character #2 - YOUNG FEMALE (TEEN - TWENTIES)

#1	YOU'RE IMPROVING
#9	FROM THE EDGE
#11	STARLET O'HARA
#21	BREAKING UP #2
#23	FIRST IMPRESSION #1
#30	ISABELLA ALESSO - JANUARY 17, 1937
#32	ISABELLA ALESSO - JANUARY 18, 1937
#49	THE MALL

Character #3 - ADULT MALE (THIRTIES - FORTIES)

#3   STUFF OF LIFE
#6   BAD SIDE
#15   COLLEGE
#25   THE BACKSIDE OF YOUR HEAD
#29   YOU CAN PICK YOUR FRIENDS...
#31   DETECTIVE GREEN - JULY 29, 2006
#33   DETECTIVE GREEN - JULY 29, 2006 #2
#44   CUTS
#48   NO SOUND TV

Character #4 - ADULT FEMALE (THIRTIES - FORTIES)

#4   SPACE #1
#5   SPACE #2
#13   SUBSCRIPTIONS
#18   B. I. Y. A.
#22   FIRST IMPRESSION #1
#27   THE TROUBLE WITH TWO
#34   STARLET KONG
#35   SPACE #3
#42   INTELLIGENCE

Character #5 - ADULT MALE (FORTIES AND UP)

#10   ROPE
#16   PERFUME AND PEANUTS
#17   THE REAL SANTA
#28   WHITE SILHOUETTE
#38   A CRIMINAL MIND
#41   ONE ON ONE
#45   X
#47   CHICKEN
#51   WELCOME TO THE JUNGLE

Character #6 - ADULT FEMALE (FORTIES AND UP)

ADDENDUM #2

SHORTER MONOLOGUES FOR AUDITIONS

ADDENDUM #3

FEMALE MONOLOGUES

ADDENDUM #4

MALE MONOLOGUES

Addendum #5 - MONOLOGUE ATTRIBUTES AND EMOTIONAL OBJECTIVE

MONOLOGUE	GENRE	GENDER/AGE RANGE	ACTING OBJECTIVE	EMOTION	PROPS	OTHER
Prologue	Drama	Open	To Intrigue To Charm	Prologue Anticipation	Card Deck	None
#1 You're Improving	Comedy	Young Female	To Reach Out	Loneliness Despair	Apron	None
#2 Conservation	Comedy	Young Male Teen – 20's	To Question	Wonder	Coffee Cup	None
#3 The Stuff of Life	Comedy	Adult Male 30's	To Challenge	Acceptance	None	None
#4 Space #1	Comedy	Adult Female 30's	To Cajole To Convince	Joy	Yellow Pad	None
#5 Space #2	Comedy	Adult Female 30's	To Cajole To Convince	Fear versus Confidence	Clip Board	Link to #5 and #35
#6 Bad Side	Drama	Adult Male 30's – 40's	To Control	Independence Indignation	None	Link to #4 and #35
#7 Crime	Drama	Young Male Teen – 20's	To Grieve To Warn	Sadness Anger	None	Singing Required
#8 Memory Pain and Truth	Drama	Adult Female 40's and up	To Inform To Deny			None
#9 From the Edge	Comedy	Young Female Teen – 20's	To Confide	Fear then Relief	French Beret	French Dialect

MONOLOGUE	GENRE	GENDER/AGE RANGE	ACTING OBJECTIVE	EMOTION	PROPS	OTHER
#10 Rope	Drama	Adult Male 40's and up	To Revere Ackowledge	Gratitude Sadness	Rope Section	None
#11 Starlet O'Hara	Comedy	Young Female Teen – 20's	To Build To Solidify To Tease	Elation Surprise	Sun Glasses	None
#12 Guys Like Stooges Girls Like Lucy	Drama	Young Male Teen – 20's	To Dominate	Sarcasm Anger	None	None
#13 Subscriptions	Comedy	Adult Female 30's – 40's	To Convince To Condescend	Confidence	Magazine	English Dialect
#14 Two Kinds of People	Comedy	Adult Female 40's and up	To Mock	Envy	Rag	Short Length
#15 College	Drama	Adult Male 30's	To Validate then Question	Acceptance Irritation	None	None
#16 Perfume and Peanuts	Comedy	Adult Male 40's and up	To Avoid	Annoyed	Paper Bag Sandwich	None
#17 The Real Santa	Comedy	Adult Male 40's and up	To Wonder	Anticipation Fear	None	None
#18 B.Y.I.A	Comedy	Adult Female 30's- 40's	To Admit To Acknowledge	Appreciation Relief	Grocery Bag	None

Monologue	Genre	Gender/Age Range	Acting Objective	Emotion	Props	Other
#19 The Way He Put Jelly on Bread	Drama	Adult Female 40's and up	To Remember	Friendship Love	None	Long Length
#20 Breaking Up Male	Comedy	Young Male Teens – 20's	To Belittle To Deny	Anger Calmness	None	Link to #21
#21 Breaking Up Female	Comedy	Young Female Teens – 20's	Hope Despair	Hope Despair	None	Link to #20
#22 First Impression 1	Comedy	Young Female Teen – 20's	To Change	Attraction Excitement	None	Link to #23
#23 First Impression 2	Comedy	Adult Female 30's – 40's	To Analyze To Conclude	Patience Acceptance	None	Link to #22
#24 I Want to be Like An Indian	Comedy	Young Male Teen – 20's	To Enlighten To Romanticize	Hope Amusement Joy	Indian Feather	Dancing
#25 The Backside of Your Head	Comedy	Adult Male 30's – 40's	To Reveal	Surprise Contentment	Two Small Mirrors	Short Length
#26 Dogs Feet Smell Like Popcorn	Comedy	Adult Female 40's and up	To Ponder To Conclude	Wonder Joy Acceptance	None	None
#27 The Trouble with 2	Drama	Adult Female 30's – 40's	To Show To Illustrate	Discovery Tolerance Respect	None	Lyric Poetry

MONOLOGUE	GENRE	GENDER/AGE RANGE	ACTING OBJECTIVE	EMOTION	PROPS	OTHER
#28 White Silhouette	Drama	Adult Male 40's and up	To Show, To Persuade, To Cajole	Desire	None	Lyric Poetry
#29 You Can Pick Your Friends...	Comedy	Adult Male 30's – 40's	To Illustrate, To Reveal, To Inform	Indignation, Discovery	Potted Plant	None
#30 Isabella Alesso – January 17, 1937	Drama	Young Female Teen – 20's	To Prepare, To Seek Perfection	Excitement, Anticipation	Diary Book Pencil	NY 30's Dialect, Linked to #'s 30, 32, 33
#31 Detective Green – July 29, 2006	Drama	Adult Male 30's – 40's	To Escape Boredom, Inattentive	Anger, Boredom	None	NY Dialect, Linked to #'s 30, 32, 33
#32 Isabella Alesso – January 18, 1937	Drama	Young Female Teen – 20's	To Prepare, To Wonder	Joy, Anticipation	Diary Book Pencil	NY 30's Dialect
#33 Detective Green – July 29, 2006	Drama	Adult Male 30's – 40's	To Discover, To be committed	Attentive, Committed, Angry	None	Linked to #'s 30, 31, 33, NY Dialect
#34 Starlet Kong 1933	Comedy	Adult Female 30's – 40's	Patience, To accept	Joy, Jealousy, Excitement	Telegram	Linked to #'s 30, 31, 32, NY Uptown Dialect

Monologue	Genre	Gender/Age Range	Acting Objective	Emotion	Props	Other
#35 Space #3	Comedy	Adult Female 30's – 40's	To Sell Hope To Show	None	Clip Board	Linked to #'s 4,5
#36 Help Wanted We're Desperate	Comedy	Adult Female 40's and up	To Unravel To Investigate	Fear Paranoia	Cell Phone or Pone	None
#37 Donuts	Comedy	Young Male Teen – 20's	To Challenge To Acknowledge	Fear Remorse	Donut	Short Length
#38 A Criminal Mind	Comedy Drama	Adult Male 40's and up	To Confess	Humility Sadness Vulnerability	Donut	Linked to #37
#39 Early Bird Special	Comedy	Adult Female 40's and up	To Analyze To Challenge	Modesty Amusement Resolution	None	None
#40 Coffee People	Comedy	Young Male Teen – 20's	To Define To Worship	Clarity Calmness Joy	Coffee Cup	None
#41 One on One	Drama	Adult Male 40's and up	To Severe To humiliate	Disappointment Constraint Obligation Cruelty	Sheet of Paper Pencil	Physicality
#42 Intelligence	Drama	Adult Female 30's – 40's	To Discover To Resolve To seek Revenge	Pain Loss Revenge	Shirt	Smell

Monologue	Genre	Gender/Age Range	Acting Objective	Emotion	Props	Other
#43 Exploring Whiteness	Comedy Drama	Adult Female 40's and up	To Decipher To Join	Confusion Negativity Confidence	None	None
#44 Cuts	Drama	Adult Male 30's – 40's	To Create Clarity	Understanding Confusion Frustration	Newspaper	None
#45 "X"	Comedy	Adult Male 40's and up	To Correct To Try but not succeed	Embarrassment	Small Fancy Shopping Bag	None
#46 Goodbye	Drama	Young Male Teens – 20's	To Feel To Reveal a fear	Fear Kindness Vulnerability	None	None
#47 Chicken	Drama	Adult Male 40's and up	To Remember To Honor	Loss Grieving Hope	None	West Virginia Dialect
#48 No Sound TV	Comedy	Adult Male 30's – 40's	To Confront To Challenge	Annoyance Completion	None	Physicality – running in place Physicality
#49 The Mall	Comedy	Young Female Teen – 20's	To Desire To Ritualize	Compulsion	None	None
#50 Creative Hiding	Comedy	Young Male Teen – 20's	To Hide To Reveal	Shy Forgetful	Shoe	None
#51 Welcome to the Jungle	Drama	Adult Male 40's and up	To Warn To Make Safe	Concern Vulnerability	None	None

MONOLOGUE	GENRE	GENDER/AGE RANGE	ACTING OBJECTIVE	EMOTION	PROPS	OTHER
#52 52 Pick Up – Epilogue	Drama	Adult Female 40's and up	To conclude, To come to an end and see	Discovery Sadness Completion	None	Lyric Poetry

BONUS MONOLOGUES -

MONOLOGUE	GENRE	GENDER/AGE RANGE	ACTING OBJECTIVE	EMOTION	PROPS	OTHER
Barber Shop	Drama	Open	To Remember what no longer exists	Discovery Happiness	None	None
Bird on a Spire	Lyric Drama	Open	To Begin	Inspiration Sadness	None	Lyric Poetry
To be Thankful Snapshots	Drama	Open	To Acknowledge	Happiness	Snapshot	None

ADDENDUM #6

USING THIS TEXT TO CREATE A LIVE THEATRICAL PRODUCTION

Production Presentation

The collection may also be used as a full length script for a live theatrical presentation or film production with the title FIFTY TWO PICKUP. The monologues, in both verse and prose, are connected thematically as parts of life and time jumbled together like a deck of cards. Fifty-two cards in a deck and fifty-two weeks in a year of a life. The collection can be assembled as a college level or professional production with minimal sets, props and lighting requirements. I have divided Production Presentation into two types with the assumption that all productions will be presented in a professional manner with careful attention to all elements of live theatrical performance including: acting, lighting, setting, use of music and direction. The reason for the division is not that one type of production is better than the other. But rather, that their purposes are quite different.

COLLEGE PRODUCTION

(As a tool for learning)

A college production purpose is to expand the performance techniques of the students and afford them experience working in front of a live audience. The manuscript has been designed to provide flexibility in assigning roles to college students of all levels. For students with entry level performance skills, there are shorter monologues which address concerns of nervousness, physicality and line memorization:

#14	TWO KINDS OF PEOPLE
#22	FIRST IMPRESSION #1
#23	FIRST IMPRESSION #2
#24	I WANT TO BE LIKE AN INDIAN
#25	THE BACKSIDE OF YOUR HEAD
#26	DOG's FEET SMELL LIKE POPCORN
#27	THE TROUBLE WITH TWO
#28	WHITE SILHOUETTE
#35	SPACE #3
#37	DONUTS
#40	COFFEE PEOPLE
#46	GOODBYE
#50	CREATIVE HIDING
#51	WELCOME TO THE JUNGLE

To Expand Performance Technique

For intermediate and advanced students, there are three instances of monologues which are linked together within a single plot line. These monologues provide an opportunity for the student actors to create characters that react to certain stimuli and evolve as the play progresses. These linked monologues are:

#30	ISABELLA ALESSO - JANUARY 17, 1937
#32	ISABELLA ALESSO - JANUARY 18, 1937

Why are there no leads?

After learning how to do something from a professional and technical perspective, the next best is to actually practice doing what you've been told and shown. It is hard for many college students (especially undergraduates) to get large roles in Theatre productions. The more common practice is to have the Graduate students play most of the lead roles and the undergraduates to take the smaller or supernumerary parts and work their way up. The idea behind this practice is to watch and learn. I am of the school of *do and learn*. 52 PICKUP has been designed to be presented as an ensemble production which has no leads or supernumeraries. Every character in the play is a lead. In this way, students participating in this production will have the opportunity to create many different characters within the production. All participants in the production will have significant stage time in order to learn their craft and become a better actor.

Creation of an Ensemble in an Educational Setting

The teacher director will have a finite pool of students to cast from: a particular class, workshop or group of students rather than conducting an open casting session from a much larger acting community. Casting is always a challenge in college productions because of the character structure of most plays, the teacher director is often forced to assign roles unevenly or without regard to a specific student's skill level or experience. The modular structure of 52 PICKUP will allow the teacher director to assign roles more evenly so that most of the students will be given enough material to challenge their creative skills and provide a realistic performance experience. Rather than create a production with traditional leads and supporting cast, the goal should be to create a working ensemble of actors working together to create the play as a whole rather than a small group of lead performers and support cast.

PROFESSIONAL PRODUCTIONS

A professional production may be presented for a number of reasons including: a **showcase for casting or artistic representation to market the talents of actors** or as a **work of art in its own merit for a general audience**. A Professional Production can have one or all of these goals.

SHOWCASE FOR CASTING OR ARTISTIC REPRESENTATION

Marketing of Talent

Actors are always looking for new ways to make their talent known to those individuals who can help them find professional work. Whenever, they perform professionally, Producers, Casting Directors and Agents are usually invited to view the actor's work in a production. However, the actor is limited by the parts they play within those productions, the location of the venue and the availability to Producers, Casting Directors or Agents to attend.

The actor also has no control of the total production and by extension the outcome of the experience. In these cases, actors often participate in showcase presentation which are presented for the specific purpose of inviting Producers, Casting Directors and Agents. The productions are usually shorter in length and are geared to market the specific talents of each actor who participates in them.

Using 52 PICK UP as a Showcase Presentation

If part of the text is used as the matrix for a showcase, the monologues assigned to the performers should be appropriate for their age range and gender. This is essential because casting directors or artistic representatives will want to see the actor performing the type of characters they would be cast in for a particular film, television show or play. It would not be wise to have actors play outside of their general acting type.

What is type?

In casting or artistic representation an actor's type takes into consideration his/her look with regard to age, gender, ethnicity, vocal quality, physicality and general demeanor or personality. You may think to yourself. I'm an actor. I can play anyone. But the truth of it is, in casting, the actor (especially an unknown) will be cast according to who they are as well as what they can do with a script. With this in mind, any production of 52 PICKUP presented as a showcase, should first and foremost take into consideration appropriate casting.

How Does a Showcase Production Work?

A showcase is a live theatrical presentation which is designed for the sole purpose of showcasing the talents of the performers with the presentation to casting personal, producers and artistic representative (agents and managers). A showcase has some of the qualities of a traditional live theatrical performance including (lighting, costume, music).

However, it is presented in an abbreviated format and is usually followed by a meet and greet where the performers may talk the attendees. In addition, the actor usually provides pictures, resumes and contact information in the lobby for showcase attendees to pick up after the presentation. What makes a showcase different is that it's sole purpose is to showcase the talents of the performers for work or representation. It is not a traditional theatrical performance with clearly defined acts and intermission.

Presenting A Showcase

A showcase presentation should be approximately one hour to an hour and half in length (including scene changes). The goal in a showcase is to give the audience (casting personnel, agents and producers) a sample of your talent, you don't have to present the whole play.

AS AN ARTISTIC PRESENTATION FOR A GENERAL AUDIENCE

Let's put on a show

52 Pickup can be developed for the sole purpose of putting on a live theatrical production for a general audience. The production from this perspective will not have an educational or marketing slant and will be directed solely toward the presentation of a live theatrical event.

Creation of a Unified Concept

If the full text is used as the material for a live theatrical presentation for a general audience, it is important to create a production incorporating one unified concept rather than present the work as a grouping of individual monologues. The production can be presented in the two act format with an intermission break between monologue #26 (DOG's FEET SMELL LIKE POPCORN and monologue #27 THE TROUBLE WITH TWO. The audience will be presented one full production unified by theme.

What is the thematic structure of 52 PICKUP?

As with most works of theater, the thematic structure can be widely interpreted by the director and ensemble. However, the most prevalent thematic thread behind the collection is that we are not alone. True, we are all dealt our own set of circumstances (cards) which, when assembled together as one, become our life. But, we don't have to make that journey alone.

Marking each step from beginning to end
not in parade
but in forgotten moments
each vanishing as it came

a stolen season
in want of repeat

Lastly, it is essential that the individual monologue segments be presented in a manner in which one section flows into the other. It is best to avoid ending all monologue segments with a blackout. It is a better idea for some of the monologues to flow into one another having one character exiting as another enters the space or using music to transition one segment to another. Ultimately, any full production of the text as a play be fifty two individual parts that are connected to one another like the pieces of a mosaic creating one total experience the audience can share with the performers.

GENERAL PRODUCTION CONSIDERATIONS

Whether the play is presented as a college or professional production, the following consideration should be addressed:

STAGING REQUIREMENTS

What kind of performance space do you have?
The play is not one of setting and spectacle, but rather one of language, physicality and emotion. With that in mind, the text has been designed for minimal setting and can work in four different formats for production:

Proscenium Staging
This traditional form of staging places the audience on one

side and the performers on another side of the action. This format lends itself, the most out of the four, to the use of simplified setting which can consists of either electronically projected or placard images to accompany some or all of the monologue presentations. The placards can contain the title of each monologue and can be carried on by the performer or stage person and placed on a easel before each presentation.

Thrust Staging

The Thrust form of staging places the audience on the three sides of the performance action. This format lends itself to smaller set pieces and simultaneous exits and entrances between monologue presentations. Performers may enter the stage space from either side of the stage as well as the audience area. In addition, this type of staging will bring the performance closer to the audience creating a more intimate atmosphere for presentation.

Arena or Round Staging

The Arena or Round form places the audience on four sides of the performer creating an intimate atmosphere for presentation. The downside of this format is that particular attention must be given in blocking the performer's movements upon the stage. At any given moment in the presentation, at least on part of the audience will not be able to see the performer's face. Careful attention should be given to opening up the action so that each monologue is presented each of the four sides of the audience area.

Environmental Staging

The environmental form of staging eliminates the distinction between a performance and audience area. The creation of one unified space encourages audience interaction between performers and audience as well as an intimate environment for presentation. If this type of setting is utilized, it is important to place the entire action within one frame. For example, a dinner party where the setting is a room in a home. The audience and performers come together within this setting and the individual monologues are presented as conversations at this event.

EQUIPMENT REQUIREMENTS -

Do you need special equipment?

No special equipment is required to produce 52 PICKUP as a full performance. However, optional equipment that can be utilized includes:

Lighting equipment

Lights can be a very expensive proposition in theatrical production. At a minimal level, you can have a clearly lit general performance area and a separate darkened audience area. However, if your space is equipped with theatrical lights, you can light several different areas of the performance area so that monologues can be presented in a textured format. You can utilize different lit areas for certain characters or monologue genres. In addition, lit areas can be defined in relationship to the audience either closer or farther within the proscenium or thrust formats. It can be faded in and out to create light and dark spaces for monologues performed within the audience areas.

Sound equipment

Utilized to provide background music for certain monologues or monologue transitions. A piano or other musical instrument can also be used for these purposes. Due to the intimate nature of the text, performers would not use microphones. Music can be used most effectively as a the glue which binds the monologues together within one unified thematic structure.

Visual Equipment

The visual aspect of the production can be as simple as placing enlarged photographs on an easel during several of the monologues. In addition, using a an easel, placards indicating the title of each monologue can be placed on the stage at the start of each monologue. A more elaborate system can be utilized using rear projections, slides or pre recorded segments to augment each monologue. The script does not require these special effects and generally they should be avoided unless you have the technical personnel available.

YOUR PRODUCTION TEAM

Like all theatrical productions, a production team of individuals should be created to support what the audience eventually will see on the stage. Often, on college campuses, this is done by the very same students that appear in the production. While there are no hard, fast rules pertaining to who does what, here is a general breakdown of a production team.

Producer

The producer is the creative force behind the production. In a college setting, this can be the professor that teaches the class. In a professional setting, this can be the person who initially conceives the production and takes it to the stage. In some definitions, the Producer is seen as the person who provides the financial backing for a given production. While this can be true in some professional productions, 52 PICKUP has been designed to done with little or no initial production costs.

DIRECTOR

The director provides the artistic point of view for the production very much the way a chef prepares a meal. The director creates an artistic vision for the material and then creates an artistic team to fulfill this vision. The artistic team created are those individuals who make up the production: actors, designers and technicians. The director usually is the final word pertaining to all artistic aspects of your production. In a college setting, this can be the professor who teaches the class, a graduate student or the chairperson of the department. In professional production, this person could be an artist for hire, an artistic director or one or more of the actors.

Director's Assistant or Production Assistant

Not a hard fast requirement but a nice person to have to address all of the multiple complexities of putting on a production. As theater is a collaborative art, it brings together many different types of people who may have different requirements to get their job done in relationship to the production. This person, with the Director's approval, is empowered to handle many of the day to day production type of duties required in presenting a production including assistance in rehearsals, scheduling, documentation of blocking, coordination of meetings or general organizational duties. In a college setting, this person can be a member of the class or a graduate student, or intern. Often, this person doubles as the *Stage Manager*, once the production is up and running. In a professional setting, the Director's Assistant does all of the duties previously described and can also work with performers by running lines, rehearing already set blocking, or working with performers who are the understudy for a particular role.

Designers:

The Visual and Auditory aspects of your production

52 PICKUP can be presented in a classroom, studio or workshop format where visual and auditory aspects of the presentation are minimal. For example, in some acting classes, the lights are general spots which are turned on and off, the audio is a CD player and the costumes are personal items provided by individuals in the workshop. However, a full theatrical production should, depending upon budget and production requirements, consider some of the following types of individuals as part of the creative team.

Set Designer

The quick definition of this person is the person who creates the sets. However, this person should really be thought of as the person who creates the environment that the production will be presented within. The play 52 PICKUP must be set in one general space that can accommodate the reality, time and place of each monologue. In addition, the Set Designer will create an environment which will take into consideration the type of staging that is available. In a college setting, this person can be a member of the faculty or graduate student who is familiar with the physical elements of the performance space and the resources available within the department or school. In a professional setting, this person is often hired by the director and creates an environment that meets the Director's specifications for a particular budget. This person can also be an actor who is a member of a professional company. In any case, this person must be familiar with the appropriate materials and construction techniques to insure that the Setting created is safe for both the performers and audience.

Costume Designer

The quick definition of this person is the person who creates the costumes. However, this person should really be thought of as the person who creates the overall character look for the production. Each monologue has its own reality, time and place which must be visually connected to the play as a whole. This can be created by having all the performers wear one general set or color of clothing, which can have individual costume pieces such as hats, scarves, glasses, ties etc within each monologue. In a college setting, the Costume Designer may really be a Costume Puller who draws all of the costumes from the college costume shop. This person can be a faculty member or student who is familiar with what the school has in its costume shop. The Costume Designer may also construct or purchase specific costumes or costume parts required for individual monologues. These type of items can include a police badge, weapon or period riding whip. Fortunately, 52 PICKUP relies on contemporary clothing and has a minimum of props. In a professional setting, the costume designer creates a look for the show in coordination with the Director's point of view for the production. This person may pull or create new costumes for the production subject to budgetary restraints.

Lighting Designer

This person creates, with the Director, the mood of the production by developing a lighting design using existing lighting or renting/purchasing additional lighting equipment. It is essential that this person is familiar with lighting equipment and its safe installation within the performance space. In a college setting, this person can be either a faculty member or student who is familiar with the space requirements and the equipment available at the school. In a professional setting, the lighting designer, creates a visual look for the performance space in coordination with the Director's point of view for the production within budgetary restraints.

Sound/ Music Designer or Music Director

This person creates, in conjunction with the Director, the auditory mood of the production by recording music to be used as part of the presentation. Music selected can be used under the performance of a particular monologue or be used during monologue transitions. In a college setting, this person can be a member of the faculty or a student who is familiar with different types of recorded and live music. In a professional setting, this person works closely with the Director to create the appropriate sound for the production within budgetary restraints. This person would also be responsible for obtaining permission to use each of the recorded tracks and provide the appropriate credits in the program.

Stage Manager

(Also see Director's Assistant or Production Assistant)
The Stage Manager is the person who runs the production once it has opened. This person assists in the rehearsals, warm ups, prompting, setting call times, and generally insuring the smooth backstage operation of the production. The Stage Manager also signals the production to begin and sets performers for entrances during production. In a college setting, this person is usually a student who has served as the Director's Assistant. In a professional setting, this person is an important part of the production and takes over the operation of the production once it has opened and the director has left.

Make Up Artist

This person is an optional part of your team. Depending upon your performance configuration you may want to have very light makeup to strengthen the features and add a bit of color of a particular actor. In most cases, each actor can do their own makeup. However, due to the intimate nature of this play and that actors should be playing within their own character age and type, make up should be used to a minimum.

General Crew or Technical People

These are the individuals who actually man the various aspects of the production. The number of technical staff varies with the complexity of your production. They may just perform some rudimentary functions such as operation of the lighting board and sound equipment or may be required to place props or move set pieces on an off the set. In a college setting, these people are normally students who (for college credit or to fulfill an hourly requirement) will sign up to provide technical support for your production. It is essential that these individual be professional and responsible when performing their support function. Their attention must be focused on the production, they must be quiet back stage and conduct their duties in a manner that is safe.

The House Manager and Ushers

The House Manager is responsible for the operation of the theater house including opening the house to the public, communication with the Stage Manager when everyone is seated, helping audience members get to their seats. In short, the House Manager is to the house what the Stage Manager is to the backstage area. This person coordinates the Ushers. These physically assist the audience in finding their seat, collect tickets and disperse programs. Ushers also keep order and resolve issue pertaining to the audience and seating. In a college setting, these positions are almost always students who are seeking college credit or hours. In a professional setting, these people may be members of the Theater Company or individuals hired by the theater to perform this function.

NOW YOU HAVE YOUR PRODUCTION TEAM WHAT ABOUT THE CAST?

THE CASTING PROCESS

The casting process for 52 PICK UP differs slightly than a traditional play because the Director has more latitude in assigning roles. The play does not have the traditional Protagonist and Antagonist nor are there major and minor roles. The cast is more of an ensemble than a grouping of major and minor roles. The good news here is that everyone can (if the Director so wishes) can have a major role.

Setting Goals for Casting:
Depending on the type and purpose of your production, you will want to set specific goals for casting:

What Kind of Production Do You Have?
As discussed earlier, your production can be for Educational Purposes, as a Showcase of Talent or as a Presentation for a General Audience or any combination of these. The type of production you have will have a direct bearing upon your casting strategy.

What is the available talent pool?

If the production is produced within an educational setting, the talent pool may be limited to the College Theater Department, Liberal Arts Program or Campus. The casting also could be composed of members of a particular studio, class or company of actors. In each case, the Producer and Director should develop a casting strategy which takes into account the available talent pool that they must draw from in order to create an ensemble. The Director may also take skill level into consideration and choose to give the more experienced students a larger share of the dialogue.

Age and Gender

In a particular casting pool, the Director may be faced with the challenge of too many females or a specific age range (ages 20-25) The age and gender breakdowns of the characters are suggested and can be altered to fit the Director's vision for the production and available talent pool. There are also bonus monologues included in the text which are not age or gender specific which can be used to create an ensemble to reflect the available talent pool.

Casting for Educational Production

When casting the production in an educational setting, the Director (Teacher or Student) should take into account the specific acting challenges each student performer is working on within the class, program or department. This Director, can reference **the attribute section of this text** as a guide to specific acting related connections to each monologue.

Casting for a Showcase Production:

When casting a showcase production, the physical make up of the cast should be varied so that there are no major *type* conflicts.

What is Type?

Type is a general description attributed to an actor in relationship to the kinds of roles an actor can play. It takes into consideration the actor's total outward appearance including: age, gender, physical stature, vocal quality, speech patterns and general demeanor. While there are no specific list of types, examples might include:

Romantic Lead

Usually attributed to a young handsome or physically attractive actor or actress.
Example Monologues: Memory Pain and Truth, From the Edge, First Impression

Character Actor:

Actors who usually play, not a lead but a supporting role in a given genre.
Example Monologue: Bad Side, Crime, Help Wanted

Streetwise Actor:

Actors who play characters who live or work on the streets and have a kind of streetwise demeanor.
Example Monologue: Detective Green, Criminal Mind

Comic Character:

Actors who are best at characters who are in absurd situation or who have certain quirks in their persona.
Example Monologues: I Want To Be Like An Indian, Coffee People, Space.

Careful attention should be made when assembling a group of actors for a showcase presentation. The desired goal, when possible, is to have a showcase ensemble which is varied with no duplication of type. The ideal situation is to present the Producer, Casting Director or Agent with many different choices of actors without duplication of type. Remember, this is not always possible because of the available types for a particular showcase production. In the case where there is duplication, it is a good idea to try to vary the styles and performances by choosing selections from the text that are the most varied.

Casting for Professional Production

The goal of casting for a professional production geared toward a general audience should be to find the best possible cast that will successfully convey the message of the play to a paying audience. It should also be a cast has the ability to reach out to an audience and be believable within each character.

Casting for Box Office:
It is no secret in Professional Theatrical or Motion Picture production that a recognizable name above the title will do more for box office than excellent reviews or positive word of mouth. I am not suggesting that you contact the agents of every movie star in Hollywood to have their clients star in your production. First of all, you might not have the budget and secondly the play lends itself to an ensemble rather than a star driven vehicle. With that said, your local community may have a well known personality or actor living within your boundaries, that you may be able to participate in your production. You can assign this person a single or multiple monologues that you deem appropriate for them to perform and like the movie producers in Hollywood, you can place this local celebrity's

name above *your* title. Another method, producers in local theatre use for increase box office is to create a larger cast for the production. This can be done in two ways, you can assign fewer monologues to each actor or you can double cast. In each case, the larger number of performers in the cast of the production the large the turnout of audience.

How to announce and Set up an Audition:

Once the casting goals established, the following steps should be taken to create an ensemble.

Creating a Casting Breakdown:
A Casting Breakdown should be created with the following information:
Name of the Production:
52 Pick UP - (A unique collection of 52 original contemporary monologues ranging in length from one to four minutes.)
Venue:
Where the production will take place –Theatre Name
Creative Team:
Producer, Director (Names of individuals)
Rehearsal Start date:
Start Date
Opening Date:
Date that your production will open to the public and length of Rune and number of performances.
Production Entity:
The Name of School, Department or Theater Company
Audition Location:
Address of audition.
Audition Time:
State specific times if an open call or phone number to set

audition appointment.

Additional Information:

Contact number or state no phone calls.

Call Back Date:

Dates and times if applicable

Special notes of preparation:

Prepare a one minute monologue. Perform monologue from script - *Sides* will be available either through a service or at the audition.

Casting for ensemble the following roles:

Character #1 - YOUNG MALE (TEEN - TWENTIES)

Character #2 - YOUNG FEMALE (TEEN - TWENTIES)

Character #3 - ADULT MALE (THIRTIES - FORTIES)

Character #4 - ADULT FEMALE (THIRTIES - FORTIES)

Character #5 - ADULT MALE (FORTIES AND UP)

Character #6 - ADULT FEMALE (FORTIES AND UP)

Pulling Sides For your Audition - What are Sides?

Sides are printed sections from the text that you will utilize at the audition. The number available sides for a traditional production is driven by the characters in the play. However, in this production, you may select any number of monologues which you feel will give you an idea of what the actor can do. Sides can be made available at the time of audition. This is okay, to get a general idea of what an actor can do. A better method would be to make the sides available through any one of the internet services that provide this service. (The Go Between, Showfax.com) They will make the sides available on line to actors for a nominal fee. This will allow the actors to be familiar with the material and give you a better idea of their abilities.

When To Post the Casting Breakdown?:
Generally, at least two to four weeks before the start of rehearsal. The earlier the better, to provide you with ample time for call backs and unforeseen circumstances.

Where To Post the Casting Breakdown?
This depends on your local setting. You can post both hard copy and online information, which can reach your available talent pool. In a college setting, you can post casting notices within the performing arts departments, place ads in school media outlets including newspapers, radio stations and campus television. You may also coordinate with university based organizations, clubs and alumni associations to insure a solid turn out for your auditions and potential audience later on. In a professional setting, you may post casting notices in local performing arts newspapers which list casting opportunities. In Los Angeles and New York, BACKSTAGE provides a free listing service for the posting of casting information. There are also numerous online resources for posting including:

Backstage: http://www.backstage.com/bso/index.jsp

Now Casting: https://www.nowcasting.com/index.php

The Right Cast: http://www.therightcast.com/act/?goto

Actor's Access: http://www.actorsaccess.com/

THE AUDITION

Unless the cast has be prearranged by the director, an audition will be necessary to create an ensemble. One important factor in casting is the creation of a cast that can work well together and *fits both* in energy and physical look. Most actors will attest to the fact that they can play any role, age or gender in a given script. The reality however, is that they will play not very far from their core physicality, age range and gender. The casting process is often one of mixing and matching the appropriate energy, physicality, and demeanor of an actors rather than whether or not they are talented enough to play a particular role. In an ensemble, every cast member must be individual with their own quirks and sensitivities but also must be clearly a fitting part of the whole group.

The goal of any audition is to create an atmosphere which is comfortable for the actors to perform. You want to be able to see them at their best, so that you may have the best idea possible about their talent and ability to fit into the character they read and mesh with the other performers.

PREPARING THE AUDITION SPACE:

The preparation of the audition space should not be extensive. It should be clean, well lit with (if possible) separate areas for waiting and performance.

Prepare a Waiting Area:

Adequate seating with a table containing a sign in sheet with columns for **Name, Role, Arrival time** and available sides collated by Character Name. If possible, a Production Assistant should be available to call up actors when its their turn and answer any questions they may have about the audition.

Note: The waiting area should be far enough or closed off from the actual audition area, so that the waiting actors cannot hear or see the audition that is in progress. If you are able to separate the two areas, it's a good idea to have a Production Assistant call up and escort each actor from the waiting area to the audition area.

Prepare a Talent Information sheet:

Create a short basic information sheet which actors must fill out in the waiting area. You will want to know their names, outside time commitments (i.e. work, school other productions), and contact information. Also, you might ask if they will accept an ensemble or lessor role in the production (if they are not selected for the leading role) and whether they have any technical knowledge to work back stage. One other excellent piece of information to ask for is their mailing address and email. Anyone coming into for an audition is also a potential audience member for your current and future productions. Don't forget to build an email and snail mail list.

Have Sides from the Script available for Actors

Remember, that sides are printed sections from the text that you will utilize at the audition. They should be placed on a table or other clearly marked area, for all of the roles that are being read that day of the audition. Categorize the sides, by **Character** not page number in your script. In addition, it is helpful to the actors, if the sides are printed in at least a 14 point font with character name and actions clearly marked so that they will be easier to read in performance. Note, that most actors will obtain sides either on the internet or by arriving early, so that their performance will be memorized.

However, even though the performances are from memory, many actors still like to hold the side in their hands during the audition.

The Audition Area

This is the space where it all happens and should approximate the aesthetic distance and volume that the intended final production will have. Don't audition in an intimate setting if you are planning on producing the production in a larger theatre. Try to audition in the same or similar space to your intended production. In addition, you should make the following considerations:

- It should be well lit so that the actor can see what they are reading and where they are moving. It should be free of debris, old set pieces, black boxes or old furniture from acting classes etc.
- It should have a clearly marked performance area so that the actor knows where they will sit or stand and where the casting personnel will be.

- It can contain other set pieces such as a stool, chair or black box.

CONDUCTING AN AUDITION

Again, the goal is to make the auditioning actors as comfortable as possible so that you may see them at their best. This is not to say, that performing within an audition setting does not encourage nervousness, insecurity (they are being judged), irrational behavior. You must be the calming factor that always brings things back to the center. One thing you can do that will go a long way to create a relaxed audition is to be polite. If you witness a reading that is horrible, don't just stop it in the middle and say Cut! That's enough!

Allow the performer the chance to present the piece fully. In the initial readings, select short parts of the monologues, (no more than a minute) which on the first pass will serve as a means for you to measure each actor's:

- Physicality
- Age
- Ability to memorize and handle dialogue
- Ability to create emotion
- Compatibility the other cast
- Ability to make creative choices

After, the actor has read the short selection, you can ask them to continue on to the next section or if they are not right for you, simply say Thank you and move on to the next person. Generally most auditions can be broken down into three parts:

Introduction

These moments are when the actor initially enters the space and is introduced to you by name. Often, general information is provided about the audition this is to follow and perhaps the production itself. This is a transition period, which allows both the actor and the casting person or persons to adjust to one another and space. It is also a time that you can generally take a look at the actor's physicality, vocal quality and demeanor.

The Reading

This is magic time. The moment when the reality of the casting session ends and the reality of the script and the characters begins. Whenever possible, it is always best NOT to read with the actor. You can have a Production Assistant read the lines with the actor so that you may fully experience all aspects of the audition performance. Be certain that Production Assistant reading with the actor puts some emotion into the read. It is not enough to have them just read the lines without feeling. This makes it more difficult for the actor reading to respond to the reality of the scene being performed. Try not to have two actors read together initially. You may do this later in call backs to see how individuals fit together. However, in the beginning, it's best to read one actor at a time.

The Moment After

When the reading is over, we transition back from the reality of the play script to the reality of the casting session. It's best to create a sense of completion by saying Thank you. This signifies that the reading is over. However, you may want to give notes and have them read again, depending of what you are working on and trying to achieve. You may also want to ask questions about items on their resume. All of these types of communication are fine. But, you are not required say anything evaluative about the reading itself such as Good Job! or That was Wonderful! or Not bad... Instead, just say thank you. That statement is really saying the reading is over. It doesn't mean they didn't get the role, it just means the reading is over at that moment in time.

THE CALL BACK

A call back is the process by which the casting person, director or producer may want to see a particular actor perform the material a second or third time. The purpose of most call backs is more about putting the cast together then assessing individual talent of an actor. Many times actors will be paired or grouped together to see how the fit with respect to physical attributes, energy and overall delivery. The purpose of your call back can include one or all of these reasons. However, the important thing to remember is to call back an actor for a reason rather than a whim. It might be a particular quality that you see in the first readings, or unique physical look. If you hold call backs set specific criteria for those call backs. Know what you will be looking for and try to target the call back to achieve that particular goal for an individual actor or the entire cast. Lastly, don't be afraid to have an actor switch roles. It's okay to ask an actor to read for another part even if it is for a smaller role as long as they are aware might consider them for a smaller role.

The Second Look

You may see an actor you like doing a certain role but you either don't know why you like them or you are not quite sure if they fit into the type of part you are considering them to play, so you call them back again. This type of call back is to reaffirm what you already like or to change your mind about them in the light of a new day. In either case, you should allow them to do what they did before so you can compare what you originally saw in them to what you see in them the second time.

Giving Notes

Certain call backs are not about talent but more about whether you can work with a particular actor. Are they able to take direction or are they stuck within their own interpretation of the role. You will also address, whether or not they fit into the casting choices you have already set in stone.

Making Changes

Everybody changes their mind about one thing or another in life. Theatre is no different. You may think of an actor to play a certain role, until (that is) you hear another actor do it. During the call back , you now see the actor in a different setting and character or relating in the ensemble as a totally different person. Change is good as long as it has purpose. If you just change for change sack, you will wind up with a very uneven production.

CREATING THE CAST

The Bouquet of Flowers

I once worked on a television pilot, many years ago. Once the pilot was created, it was viewed by the network (who loved it) and then promptly released all of the actors. I asked the producer: If they loved the show, why did they fire all of the actors? He smiled and said: They were looking for a certain bouquet and didn't see it. I always thought that a bouquet applied only to flowers. He explained that creating a cast is like assembling a bouquet of flowers. The creator may love each flower individually but when assembled into one grouping they may not quite fit. This was the case in my pilot. The actors simply didn't mesh into one unified cast. Each was talented in his or her own way but there was not a team. When you create your cast for a production of 52 PICK UP, take particular attention to the way they all fit together. Ask yourself, does anyone stick out either in a good or bad way from the rest of the group. If it is so, then try to find out why? If you have to make changes from your original casting choices, it's best to do it as soon as possible. Ultimately, you want to create one unified cast.

THE FIRST REHEARSAL

This is one of the most important rehearsals you will have because it is your opportunity to create the frame that will surround the picture you will paint.

Set the tone and parameters for the rehearsal

This is important. If you have a very specific concept for presenting this play and a limited amount of time. You will want to set the parameters that you have a plan and want to use the rehearsal time in its implementation. You may also want to work in a collaborative manner in which you solicit suggestions from the actors as you put the production together. If you choose this approach, set specific parameters on how this process will work or you will have a the actors all directing each other which will lead to chaos.

Set the POINT OF VIEW FOR THE PRESENTATION OF THE PRODUCTION

Also important. You need to lay out for the entire cast your vision for creating the production. If for example, you were presenting Shakespeare's ROMEO AND JULIET you could present the play many different ways including traditional

Elizabethan (Franco Zeffirelli) modernistic (Baz Lurhmann) or acrobatic (Andre Serban). The actual play script, dialogue and setting might remain the same but the manner in which the production is presented would fit into a particular interpretation or point of view. Once your cast is aware of the direction the production will take, they will align themselves to it and move toward that direction.

Administration

The Framework for how it will all happen, set the schedule and introduce the creative team.

The first rehearsal also is time to introduce the production team and actors, set schedules and present a specific calendar which shows what the cast will be doing through the rehearsal period up to the opening.

THE REHEARSAL PROCESS

The rehearsal process of any theatrical production includes the creation of an intellectual, emotional and physical frame by which the actors can experiment with the play and their characters.

Intellectual -
Exploring the Goals of each character within the play

The goals of each of the characters must be identified and set with each monologue and related to the production as a whole. The actors must gain an understanding of why the characters do what they do and say what they say. The actors need to discover what each of their characters want within each monologue and within the play itself.

Emotional -
Exploration of the character's feelings about themselves and other characters within the play

The inner feelings of each of the characters must be explored. The must discover how their characters feel about themselves and other characters within the body of each monologue and in the play as a whole.

Physical -

How the characters relate to the space, other characters and the audience

The inner physicality of each character. Actors need to discover what each character does and how they physically relate to the performance space, their individual realities and to other characters. The physical movement of the characters upon the stage is referred to as blocking. Blocking can be pre set by the director prior to rehearsal (preparation of a production book) or it can evolve organically during rehearsal and then set for lighting before the opening of the production.

Ultimately, the rehearsal process is the journey that the actors, directors and production team will make in discovering their own meaning of the play which they will convey to an audience.

OPENING NIGHT

It's never over. Just because the production opens and is viewed by an audience, it doesn't mean that the creative process ends. The production should continue to be honed and improved up until and including its last performance. The director and technical personnel should continue to work with the actors to improve and clarify the production for the audience.

THREE THINGS NOT TO FORGET WITH THEATRICAL PRODUCTION:

Keep it simple

Theater is an art form whose medium is language. Let the meaning of the play be conveyed intellectually, emotionally and physically by the actors and the words and action of the play without overusing lighting, sound and technical effects.

Be open to the creative process

The creation of a theatrical production is a journey which is based upon the collaboration of many different people including actors, designers, writers, directors and ultimately the audience. Allow yourself to take the full creative journey, be open to new ideas and constantly evaluate your own ideas.

Have fun!

Don't ever forget why you started the whole process in the first place. Find the joy in what you do and be thankful that you have the opportunity in the process of presenting a play to a live audience.

Addendum #7 -
BONUS MONOLOGUES

THE BARBERSHOP

I was just thinking about when I was a kid... my dad used to take me to the Barbershop... a modest three seat store front with one of those swirling red and white candy cane poles in front. No appointments... you just went in and had a seat. They had comic books to read until it was your turn... and when it was my turn they would straddle me on a leather bench which sat up on top of the arms of the barber's chair. When I sat up there, I was as tall as the barber. He always wore a white barber's smock which looked just like the one the pharmacist wore at the drug store... he cut my hair with scissors, made a slow line around my ears and then evened off the back with one of those electric clippers... used to tickle the back of your neck. To finish it off, he'd put some green slick which came from a bottle that looked like glue... it would go on your hair soft but after a few seconds... it was hard as a rock ... On the way out, you would get a piece of Bazooka bubble gum or a lollipop and you were out the door. That was it... done! Total simplicity...

(Beat)

The barber shop...

BLACK BIRD ON A SPIRE

I woke up one morning
early
in that quiet time
before the sun
pulls back the still
created by night

Only a rabbit stirred
the morning mist
folding it away in circles
as a curtain does at the beginning of a play
warranting our sober attention
of something greater to come
then
its first actor struts and flutters
upon the stage

a small dark shadow
of a black bird
posted itself upon a spire
which was the highest point
from where I could see
his back crested in an deep orange glow
set upon by the sun's pointed light
this haloed dark angel sang out a song
in quarter and half
calling up the day
bidding farewell to the night
and although too early for most to hear
the rabbit turned away from nibbling
long enough to crane his neck upward
toward the sound

and I
also pulled myself up from *my* comfort
to see
this black bird on a spire

SNAPSHOTS

(Holding Snapshot)

I was looking at some old snapshots the other day. Ya'know, those faded color portraits of both significant moments of your life. Birthday's, Weddings, Vacations, Graduations or nonsensical, like you with your head in a toilet bowl, wearing a funny hat or making a crazy face. Lots of poses, smiling. Cheeze! Some with people you know and some you don't. Ever ask yourself: Who is that person I have my arm around? They also could be with inanimate objects. Here I am in front of the palm tree outside of our hotel room in Hawaii... here you are in front of the palm tree... and of course... here's the palm tree alone. We take these snapshots to somehow offer proof or our passing. A sort of validated parking ticket that we existed. We walked this earth and touched the lives of those we loved... and hopefully made a difference... and then, when its finally all over. When someone finds these snapshots in a book, suitcase or dresser drawer and looks at them. Like parts of a mosaic ... they will put us together again... and remember.

Addendum # 8 -
MONOLOGUE ASSIGNMENT SHEETS

ASSIGNMENT #1

NAME:_____   Class: _____

Monologue Title:_____   Grade: _____

MONOLOGUE ATTRIBUTES:

Genre:_____

Gender/Age:_____

Objective: _____

Emotional Attribute:___ _____

Singing _____

Props?_____

Other: _____

Who Am I?

Personal:_____

Professional: _____

Private:_____

THE MOMENT BEFORE

Where has my Character Come From?

What Just Happened?

CREATING NOW

Who Am I talking to?

What is going on at This Moment?

When is this Moment in Time?

Where is your Character?

CREATING THE MOMENT AFTER

Where is Your Character Going? What's going to happen next? your character's Objectives?

Beats / Line #'s

_____   _____
_____   _____
_____   _____
_____   _____
_____   _____
_____   _____
_____   _____
_____   _____

Character's   Obstacle's?

_____   _____
_____   _____
_____   _____
_____   _____
_____   _____
_____   _____
_____   _____
_____   _____

ACTING OBJECTIVES (for classroom and studio)

What elements of acting are you working on In class?

What Are Your Acting Goals for this Assignment?

Instructor comments: _____
_____
_____
_____
_____

ASSIGNMENT #2

NAME:_____   Class: _____
Monologue Title:_____   Grade: _____

MONOLOGUE ATTRIBUTES:
Genre:_____
Gender/Age:_____
Objective: _____
Emotional Attribute:_____
Staging _____
Props?_____
Other: _____

Who Am I?
Personal:_____
Professional: _____
Private:_____

THE MOMENT BEFORE
Where has my Character Come From?

What Just Happened?

CREATING NOW
Who Am I talking to?

What is going on at This Moment?

When is this Moment in Time?

Where is your Character?

CREATING THE MOMENT AFTER

Where is Your Character Going?   What's going to happen next? your character's Objectives?

Beats / Line #'s

——————   ————————————————————————
——————   ————————————————————————
——————   ————————————————————————
——————   ————————————————————————
——————   ————————————————————————
——————   ————————————————————————
——————   ————————————————————————
——————   ————————————————————————

Character's   Obstacle's?

——————   ————————————————————————
——————   ————————————————————————
——————   ————————————————————————
——————   ————————————————————————
——————   ————————————————————————
——————   ————————————————————————
——————   ————————————————————————
——————   ————————————————————————

ACTING OBJECTIVES (for classroom and studio)

What elements of acting are you working on In class?

What Are Your Acting Goals for this Assignment?

Instructor comments: _____
_____
_____
_____
_____

ASSIGNMENT #3

NAME:_____   Class: _____

Monologue Title:_____   Grade: _____

MONOLOGUE ATTRIBUTES:

Genre:_____

Gender/Age:_____

Objective: _____

Emotional Attribute:_____

Staging _____

Props?_____

Other: _____

Who Am I?

Personal:_____

Professional: _____

Private:_____

THE MOMENT BEFORE

Where has my Character Come From?

What Just Happened?

CREATING NOW

Who Am I talking to?

What is going on at This Moment?

When is this Moment in Time?

Where is your Character?

CREATING THE MOMENT AFTER

Where is Your Character Going? What's going to happen
next? your character's Objectives?

Beats / Line #'s

———— ————————————————
———— ————————————————
———— ————————————————
———— ————————————————
———— ————————————————
———— ————————————————
———— ————————————————
———— ————————————————

Character's   Obstacle's?

———— ————————————————
———— ————————————————
———— ————————————————
———— ————————————————
———— ————————————————
———— ————————————————
———— ————————————————
———— ————————————————

ACTING OBJECTIVES (for classroom and studio)

What elements of acting are you working on In class?

What Are Your Acting Goals for this Assignment?

Instructor comments: _____
_____
_____
_____
_____

ASSIGNMENT #4

NAME:_____ Class: _____

Monologue Title:_____ Grade: _____

MONOLOGUE ATTRIBUTES:

Genre:_____

Gender/Age:_____

Objective: _____

Emotional Attribute:_____

Staging _____

Props?_____

Other: _____

Who Am I?

Personal:_____

Professional: _____

Private:_____

THE MOMENT BEFORE

Where has my Character Come From?

What Just Happened?

CREATING NOW

Who Am I talking to?

What is going on at This Moment?

When is this Moment in Time?

Where is your Character?

CREATING THE MOMENT AFTER

Where is Your Character Going?   What's going to happen next? your character's Objectives?

Beats / Line #'s

_____	_____
_____	_____
_____	_____
_____	_____
_____	_____
_____	_____
_____	_____
_____	_____

Character's   Obstacle's?

_____	_____
_____	_____
_____	_____
_____	_____
_____	_____
_____	_____
_____	_____
_____	_____

ACTING OBJECTIVES (for classroom and studio)

What elements of acting are you working on In class?

What Are Your Acting Goals for this Assignment?

Instructor comments: _____
_____
_____
_____
_____

ASSIGNMENT #5

NAME:_____ Class: _____

Monologue Title:_____ Grade: _____

MONOLOGUE ATTRIBUTES:

Genre:_____

Gender/Age:_____

Objective: _____

Emotional Attribute:_____

Stnging _____

Props?_____

Other: _____

Who Am I?

Personal:_____

Professional: _____

Private:_____

THE MOMENT BEFORE

Where has my Character Come From?

What Just Happened?

CREATING NOW

Who Am I talking to?

What is going on at This Moment?

When is this Moment in Time?

Where is your Character?

CREATING THE MOMENT AFTER
Where is Your Character Going? What's going to happen next? your character's Objectives?
Beats / Line #'s

_____	_____
_____	_____
_____	_____
_____	_____
_____	_____
_____	_____
_____	_____
_____	_____

Character's   Obstacle's?

_____	_____
_____	_____
_____	_____
_____	_____
_____	_____
_____	_____
_____	_____
_____	_____

ACTING OBJECTIVES (for classroom and studio)
What elements of acting are you working on In class?

What Are Your Acting Goals for this Assignment?

Instructor comments: _____
_____
_____
_____
_____

Made in the USA
Lexington, KY
18 September 2012